U.S. ENERGY INDEPENDENCE

A PLAN FOR ENERGY INDEPENDENCE BY 2020

WALTER R. MAY, PH.D.

SFA INTERNATIONAL, INC.

HOUSTON, TEXAS U.S.A.

Library of Congress Control Number: 2008933287

Executive Editor: Cheryl A. May
Cover Designer: Yvonne Vermillion

Copyright ©2008 by SFA International, Inc.

All rights reserved. No part of this book may be reproduced or transmitted in any form or by any means, electronic or mechanical, including photocopying, recording or by any information storage and retrieval system, without permission in writing from the publisher.

ISNB: 978-0-615-22327-8

Printed in the United States

Published in the United States of America by

SFA International, Inc.
6143 Sienna Arbor Lane
Houston, TX 77041-6038

For additional copies, contact SFA International at:
www.SFAInternational.com

Dedication

To every American who has loved and made sacrifices for our country.

Table of Contents

	Preface	v
Chapter 1	An Overview and Proposals for Energy Independence	1
Chapter 2	Increasing Oil Production in the U.S.	9
Chapter 3	Reducing Petroleum-Based Fuel Consumption in the U.S.	15
Chapter 4	Long-Term Energy Sources	33
Chapter 5	Long-Term Solutions to Reduce Energy Consumption	43
Chapter 6	Maintaining Energy Independence	53
Appendix A	U.S. Energy Supply and Use	59
Appendix B	Sources of Petroleum	63
Appendix C	U.S. Refineries and Capacities	85
Appendix D	Fuel Use by Transportation Mode	93
Appendix E	Reduction of Liquid Petroleum Fuel Consumption in Transportation	105
Appendix F	Electrical Power	115
Appendix G	Hydrocarbon Combustion Reaction Chemistry and Environmental Considerations	125
Appendix H	Economic and Consumption Effects on Oil Prices	133
	Glossary	141
	Bibliography	151
	The Author	153
Table I	Total U.S. Energy Supply and Disposition	60
Table Ia	U.S. Energy Supply and Disposition (2007)	62
Table II	World Proved Reserves of Oil (2007) - Region	66

Table of Contents (Continued)

Table IIa	World Proved Reserves of Oil (2007) - Country	69
Table IIb	World Proved Reserves of Oil (2007) - OPEC and Non-OPEC Countries	70
Table III	U.S. Oil Reserves by State	71
Table IIIa	U.S. Oil Reserves by State and Region (2006)	72
Table IIIb	U.S. Oil Reserves by Volume	73
Table IV	World Production of Crude Oil and Other Liquids	74
Table IVa	World Production of Crude Oil by Volume	77
Table IVb	World Production of Crude Oil - OPEC vs. Non-OPEC Countries	78
Table IVc	World Production by Region	79
Table V	U.S. Imports by Country of Origin - OPEC vs. Non-OPEC	80
Table Va	U.S. Imports by Country	83
Table VI	U.S. Refineries Operable Capacity	87
Table VIa	U.S. Refining Capacity by State	90
Table VIb	U.S. Refinery and Blender Net Production	91
Table VII	Transportation Sector Energy Use by Mode and Type (2001 - 2008)	97
Table VIIa	Transportation Sector Energy Use by Mode and Type (2007)	98
Table VIII	Vehicle and Population Ratios Since 1960	99
Table VIIIa	Average Vehicle Statistics	100
Table VIIIb	Number of Trucks by Weight	101
Table VIIIc	U.S. Domestic Freight	102
Table VIIId	Rail Growth Scenarios - 2020	103

Table of Contents (Continued)

Table IX	Transportation Sector Fuel Use Reduction	112
Table IXa	U.S. Energy Report	113
Table X	Comparison of Electricity Generating Cost by Fuel and Country	120
Table Xa	Net Electrical Generation by Principle Energy Source	121
Table XI	World Proved Reserves of Natural Gas, 2007	122
Table XIa	World Proved Reserves of Natural Gas, 2007 - OPEC vs. Non-OPEC	123
Table XIb	Natural Gas Reserves by U.S. State, 2006	124
Table XII	Steam Boiler and Process Heater Combustion Reactions	129
Table XIIa	U.S. Fuel Use and Carbon Dioxide Production	131
Table XIII	United States Foreign Trade Balance	137
Table XIIIa	Domestic Crude Oil Prices	138
Table XIIIb	U.S. Oil Imports Cost	139
Figure 1	U.S. Petroleum Consumption	1
Figure 2	Crude Oil Price	2
Figure 3	U.S. Balance of Payments	3
Figure 4	U.S. Crude Oil Production	9
Figure 5	U.S. Automobiles and Light Trucks	16
Figure 6	U.S. Automobiles and Light Trucks Average Fuel Consumption	17
Figure 7	Gold Price, Dollars per Ounce	134
Figure 8	Conversion Rate of Euros to U.S. Dollars	135
Map	Future (Railroad) Volumes Compared to Future Capacities in 2035 without Improvements	47

Preface

The United States is in the throes of an energy crisis. Policies leading to energy independence must be a top priority of our nation. The purpose of this book is to review the current situation and consider what is needed for the U.S. to achieve energy independence by 2020. Attaining our independence will be a challenge for every U.S. citizen and require sacrifices by all. We must learn to live within our means. Consuming more energy than we produce is a form of living on credit and will ultimately impact our ability to control our destiny. The proposals presented in this book will 'stir the pot' and promote 'out of the box' ways of resolving our current predicament. If the reader is stimulated to better understand the seriousness of the situation and consider possible solutions, the goal of this book will have been achieved.

America is fast approaching a junction in our path to the future. One path can take us to energy independence. The second path will lead us in a too familiar direction of dependence on foreign sources of petroleum with severe economic and political consequences. The latter choice will also steer us on a collision course with developing countries such as India and China.

The road to energy independence will require strong leadership. Unfortunately, too many of our leaders are governed by special interest groups. These include industrialists and environmentalists, amongst others. **Politicians, including our presidential candidates, pundits, columnists, editorial writers and energy experts all seem to look only at the short-term problem of reducing crude oil and gasoline prices. Few are taking a serious look at the root causes of high petroleum prices and what is required to attain energy independence.**

In the spring of 2008, five chief executives of major oil companies were taken before Congress and berated for high gasoline and Diesel fuel prices. Oil companies were pictured as villains taking food out of the mouths of children. The politicians trying to make a name with their grandstanding showed pitifully little knowledge about energy. Federal and state governments have contributed significantly to the increasing cost of fuels by passing laws preventing drilling in ANWR and Prudhoe Bay (Alaska North Slope), off the coasts of Florida and California and continental federal land. The EPA and state agencies have required regional and seasonal blends with ultra low sulfur levels that raise refining costs. When fuel prices escalate due to lack of production and regulations, these same politicians use the oil companies as whipping boys.

Threats are made to tax windfall profits without considering that these profits are already heavily taxed and this money must be used to help pay for expensive exploration and drilling as well as development of new energy sources including liquid fuels from coal, natural gas and shale oil.

Environmentalists have made a good case that we must cherish and nourish the world around us. Our high standard of living is based on energy. A balanced approach must be taken between achieving energy independence and caring for and protecting the environment. We cannot have every new coal or nuclear plant proposal blocked because of irrational fears regarding a safe and environmentally secure future. Concerns raised about these issues must be answered with solid science and engineering.

We can achieve energy independence in the U.S. The toughest job will be finding leaders who understand the global problem and are willing to take on special interest groups ranging from industrial lobbyists to those who prefer that we live in a simple world with minimal energy use.

The chapters of this book analyze our energy situation and present proposals in large brush strokes with a minimum of data. Hard data are presented in the appendices. Primary tables are numbered consecutively with Roman numerals. Derivative tables where data have been arranged to illustrate an observation are named with the Roman numeral of the original table followed by letters (Table I, Ia, etc.). Arabic numerals are used for figures and letters for appendices.

My most sincere thanks go to Cheryl, my CPA wife, who spent most of her career in the financial sector of the energy patch. Cheryl holds a B.S. in Business Administration, University of Wyoming and an M.S. in Accounting, University of Houston. Cheryl patiently read draft after draft and made many valuable suggestions helping to bring this information together in a coherent form. Without her, this book would not have been possible. Enjoy the humor she added to the front cover!

My heartfelt appreciation is also extended to Vicki Colhurst Kopp, B.S. Mathematics, Rice University, MBA University of Texas and M.S. Accounting, University of Houston, for her assistance in the preparation of this book. Vicki's career includes many energy projects in strategic planning and other oil and gas assignments. I would also like to recognize the valuable suggestions of Walter Cloudt, a Texas A&M graduate who has specialized on the engineering aspects of the electric power industry.

And last and most importantly, I would like to thank you, dear reader, for taking the time to read this book and consider the ideas put forth for achieving energy independence. This book addresses macro issues, but there are many additional ways that everyone can conserve precious energy in businesses, homes and in our daily lives. Readers living outside the United States should find a number of ideas applicable to your country.

Walter R. May, Ph.D.

Chapter 1

An Overview and Proposals for Energy Independence

The United States of America is facing a catastrophe of unmitigated proportions and no one seems to be taking it seriously. That catastrophe is dependence on foreign sources for one-third of our energy even though the U.S. has more than sufficient energy resources. We ask other countries such as Canada, Mexico and Saudi Arabia to supply our increasing needs rather than establishing goals and working toward an energy independent future. We are currently experiencing the beginning of this crisis. How could this have happened to a resource wealthy and powerful country like the United States? This chapter will examine the root causes and our current position. It will also propose short-term and long-term goals and what will happen if we do not respond – now! Details of these proposals will be given in the following chapters.

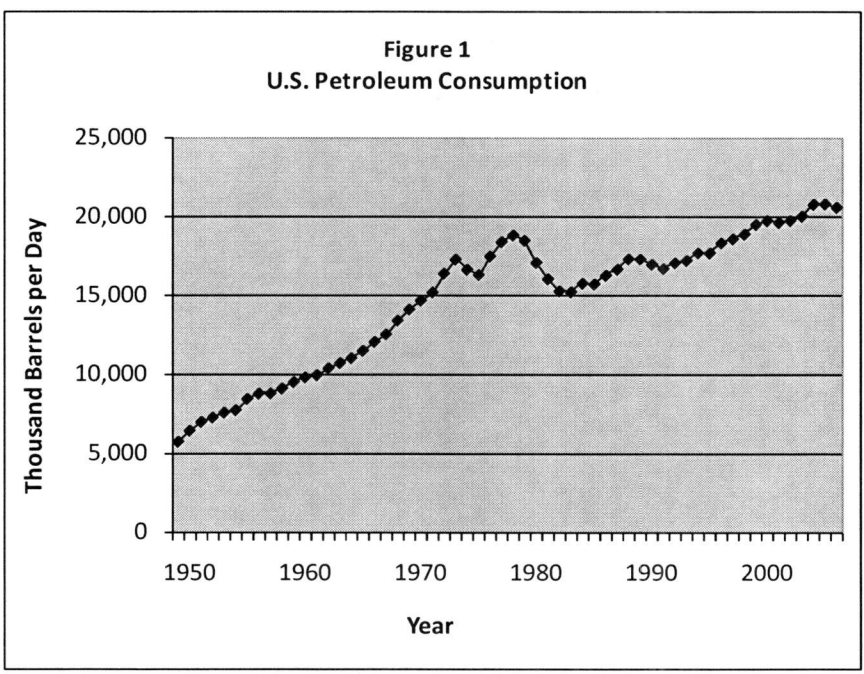

Figure 1
U.S. Petroleum Consumption

Petroleum consumption in the U.S. has increased four fold since 1950 – see Figure 1. In 2007, the U.S. consumed 101.4 quadrillion Btu's of energy. Petroleum fluids total 39.6% of energy consumption, natural gas 23.3%, coal 22.4% and nuclear power 8.2%. The remaining 6.5% came from hydropower, biomass and various renewable energy sources such as wind power. **Our imminent problem is our consumption (2007) of *imported* energy: 66% of crude and refined petroleum fuels and 16.7% of natural gas. In 2007, 29.4% of our total energy came from foreign sources[1].**

What is the forecast for 2008? The U.S. will consume about 21 million barrels of crude and refined oil products daily and import 14 million barrels of that amount. The price of crude oil is at an all time high in inflation-adjusted dollars – see Figure 2 below. Conservatively, at $120/barrel, the cost for 14 million barrels per day will be $613 billion for the year. In addition, we will import 4.66 quadrillion Btu's of natural gas at a cost of $50 billion.

We estimate that in 2008 $663 billion dollars will flow from our borders for energy purchases. Our total trade deficit in 2007 was $711 million. Adding the effect of $60/bbl increase in price of crude oil since 2007, the U.S. will have a $1 trillion dollars trade deficit in 2008.

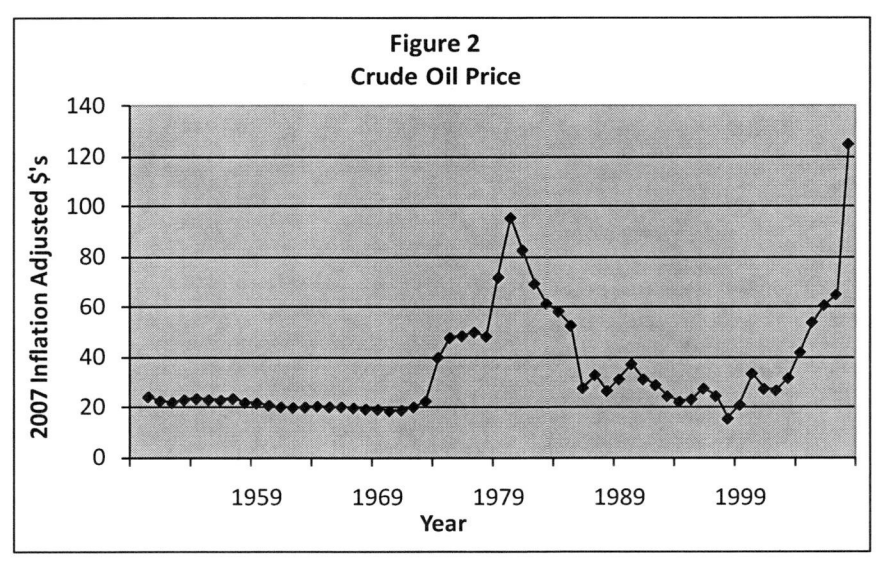

---

[1] Appendix A.

Although the deficit has been smaller in past years, the level is increasing geometrically because of the devalued dollar. The dollar has decreased in value from $0.80 per Euro to $1.56 since 2002. A U.K. pound is approximately $2.00. More importantly, the price of crude oil has not changed as much in Euros or gold as it has in dollars. **The weak dollar is a major component of the increase in crude oil price.** In the mean time, our appetite for crude oil remains unabated. Figure 3 illustrates the continued increase in our trade deficit over the past 35 years[2].

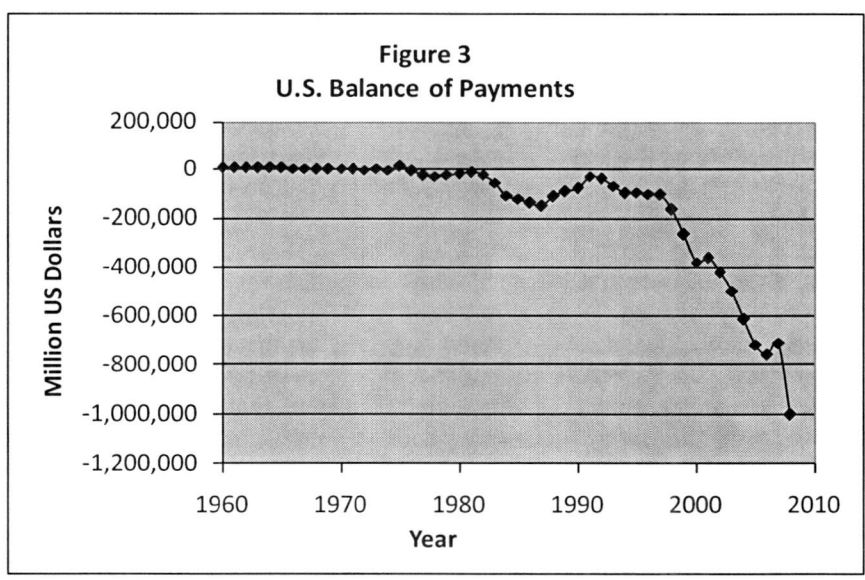

The U.S. has about 22 billion barrels of proven reserves. The U.S. ranks 12th in the world (ahead of China in 13th position) with 1.2% of total proven reserves. The U.S. will produce about 7 million barrels of crude oil per day in 2008. At this rate, proven U.S. reserves will run out in 8.5 years. Current world oil production is 86 million barrels per day. **Total world proven reserves are 1.3 trillion barrels. At this rate, these reserves will be exhausted in 42 years**[3].

World production seems to be at or near the maximum with the current production infrastructure. There are reports that the famous Ghowar field in Saudi Arabia, largest in the world and producing 5 million barrels per day, has peaked and started to deteriorate. Iran has enormous reserves, but

---

[2] Appendix H.
[3] Appendix B.

development of new fields and increased production has been inhibited due to international embargoes. Venezuela production is decreasing because of nationalization and mismanagement; current crude oil production cannot be substantially increased because of damage to geological structures. Saudi Arabia cannot significantly increase its current capacity. The Saudi's have embarked on projects such as producing aluminum that will require enormous amounts of electricity produced with crude oil. This will further decrease their capacity to supply oil to the world.

At the same time, there are no significant actions taking place in the United States to abate our appetite for oil. **China and India are rapidly coming on line as large users of crude oil, and their combined imports of oil are equal to ours and growing.** Both countries are aggressively pursuing oil all over the world. China is heavily involved in African fields and has discussed drilling for Cuba off the coast of Florida. India has recently signed trade agreements with Iran. The outlook is not rosy.

How did the U.S. sink into this situation? Our hunger for oil can be attributed to several phenomena. The first came with the economic explosion in the U.S. following World War II. Government spending on the war effort had been astronomical. During WW II, our national debt increased at a rate approaching $100 million a year, a multiple of total federal government revenue. When the war was over, there was an enormous pent up demand for goods and services of all kinds and people clamored for mobility.

During the war, General Dwight David Eisenhower studied the German autobahn system. The primary mode of transportation for freight and passengers in the U.S. during World War II was rail. Our highway system was not conducive to long range travel; trucks were slow, roads were poor and air travel was only for the very wealthy and was not very reliable. After Eisenhower became president, the National Defense Highway Act was passed and construction began on our interstate highway system. It was observed that opening an interstate highway system ended passenger service on parallel railroads.

During this same period, the technology and infrastructure of the aircraft industry was vastly improving; airplane travel became an integral part of the American lifestyle – both work and play. A major technological advance was the development of the aircraft combustion turbine engine and adaptation to commercial aviation. Piston engines were notoriously unreliable and high maintenance. It was commonplace on flights across the Atlantic to have one engine shut down on four-engine aircrafts. Combustion turbine engines provided reliability and doubled the speed of piston-engine aircraft. Flight time from New York to London was reduced from fourteen to seven hours. The first jet aircraft were introduced in 1959 and dominated commercial air travel by 1970.

Increased mobility and faster speeds had cultural and economic impacts. High capacity production lines for automobiles accompanied by attractive financing packages by banks and other lenders made the automobile widely available across all economic levels of the population. In 1970, the population of the U.S. was 200 million and there were 108 million automobiles.[4] Crude oil production in the U.S. reached 9.6 million barrels per day that year, and we domestically produced all of our energy needs including oil.

From the introduction of the first new post World War II models, U.S. automobiles were characterized by enormous, fuel inefficient engines. The author owned a 1972 station wagon equipped with a seven-liter engine. It weighed 6,000 lbs., had a 20-gallon fuel tank and consumed one gallon of gasoline every ten miles. Interestingly, it did not matter whether driving was city or highway; fuel consumption was the same.

The first glitch with fuel came in the early 1970's during the Nixon Administration when we became net importers of oil. Speed limits were reduced to a maximum of 55 mph. Gasoline prices rose to $0.40/gal. The next petroleum shock came in the late 1970's when OPEC countries embargoed crude oil in protest over U.S. support of Israel. Then, another factor came into play: OPEC and other oil producing countries had become addicted to the U.S. dollar influx into their countries. They needed dollars to pay for projects and debt; the embargo ended and oil production and prices stabilized. Meanwhile in the U.S., unhappiness with the national 55 mph speed limit led to current 70 mph and higher speed limits. Americans returned to buying high performance, heavy weight automobiles and trucks; and automobile manufacturers have been more than happy to accommodate the gluttonous tastes of their customers. And thus, consumption of petroleum has continued to spiral upward.

To support our appetite for petroleum-based fuels, the U.S. changed from an energy neutral country in 1970 to an importer of two-thirds of its petroleum requirements in 2000. What happened from 2000-2008? U.S. energy consumption has grown by 15% since 2001. As stated earlier, U.S. oil consumption in 2008 will be about 21 million barrels per day. Our total refining

---

[4] Appendix D, Table VIII.

capacity is 17 million barrels per day[5]. The result is that a significant amount of the 14 million barrels imported per day is in the form of refined product. In 2007, U.S. population reached 300 million, and we now have 230 million vehicles compared with 74 million in 1960. Gasoline consumption rose from 4 million to 9.3 million barrels per day between 1960 and 2007. Current oil production is at a worldwide level of 86 million barrels a day. As stated earlier, prospects are not bright for significant production rate increases and thus, oil prices will continue to climb.

Our economy will collapse within the next few years if we do not change our sources and uses of energy. The dollar will be severely devalued. We will not be able to purchase sufficient energy. The effect will be disastrous. We are observing the largest transfer of wealth between nations in history.

The U.S. can solve this problem, but we need to act and act now. Initiating these proposals two or four years from now will be too late. Solving our energy problems will be difficult, not because we do not have ample supplies of energy; but because **Americans have to be convinced of the need to rethink how we use energy and, in particular, our modes of transportation. Strong leadership will be needed to battle special interest groups that range from environmentalists to unions that protect jobs to industry groups that will resist changing the status quo.**

In order to reach necessary goals, our government will need to assist private industry expand technology through tax incentives and grants. Influential leaders will need to explain carefully, in detail and frequently, what we are doing and why we are doing it.

Energy independence will require sacrifices and cannot be done in a relatively short period of time. The fact that the U.S. is addressing the problem will have a salutary effect on energy markets and help stabilize the dollar. Solutions are not magical and will not be particularly easy. Most will require education on the part of our society and industry and the rethinking of priorities.

The alternative is to do nothing. The situation will resolve itself with calamitous results. The value of the dollar will continue to spiral downward. The U.S. will not be able to afford the imported crude oil and natural gas to sustain the economy. Transportation will become very difficult. Foreign money – cheap U.S. dollars – will take over our country, and we will be at the

---

[5] Appendix C.

mercy of unelected foreign leaders with no respect for our constitution and laws. This is not a world to leave to our grandchildren.

THE PLAN

Reaching energy independence will require several steps. It can be done by 2020 with concerted effort and strong leadership. Proposals for obtaining U.S. Energy Independence are both short-term and long-term. Short-term goals are those that we can begin to act on immediately. Long-term goals are those that will involve extensive planning, research and development, and infrastructure changes. Each of these goals is discussed in detail in Chapters 2 through 5.

Short-Term Goals for Energy Independence by 2020

Goal #1. Increase U.S. Petroleum Production from 7 to 14 Million Barrels per Day as an Interim Solution to Our Energy Crisis.

Goal #2. Decrease U.S. Petroleum Consumption by 20% with Conservation, Alternative Fuels, Fuel Additives and Engineering.

Long-Term Goals for Energy Independence by 2020

Goal #3. Replace All Imported Crude Oil and Petroleum Products with Domestic Production and Alternative Sources of Energy and Fuels.

Goal #4. Rebuild our Transportation Infrastructure to Use Different Sources of Energy that Permanently Replace Imported Petroleum-Based Fuels.

While the two short-term goals are challenging, both will have a significant effect on world petroleum consumption and prices. Progress on these goals will reduce our balance of payments deficit and stabilize the dollar. ***Striving to*** *meet these short-term goals will buy us time to meet the long-term goals that are critical to the future of our nation.*

In Chapter 6 we will examine steps necessary to permanently secure our celebrated energy independence.

Chapter 2

Increasing Oil Production in the U.S.

Goal #1. Increase U.S. Petroleum Production from 7 to 14 Million Barrels per Day as an Interim Solution to Our Energy Crisis.

Let us begin this chapter by examining the possibility that producing 14 million barrels per day is a realistic short-term goal until alternative fuels can be developed. This is a 100% increase over current production. It is 3 million barrels per day more than the U.S. produced at peak capacity in the 1970's. U.S. oil production has dropped steadily since the late 1980's - see Figure 4[1].

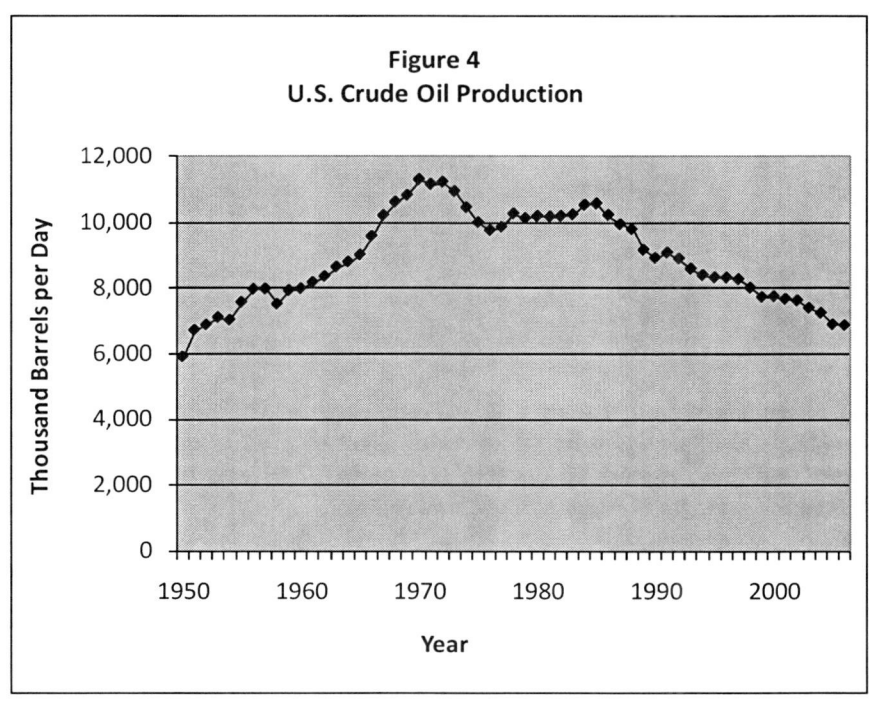

---

[1] 2006 EIA, *Petroleum Supply Monthly* (February 2007).

In January 2007, the U.S. Department of Energy[2] published proven U.S. crude oil reserves from the following sources:

Oil and Gas Journal	21.757 Billion Barrels
BP Statistical Review	29.922
World Oil	21.757

If we were to increase production to 14 million barrels per day, production would be sustainable for 4.3 years at the lower number and 5.9 years at the higher number. Based on proven crude reserves above, it would be unrealistic to pursue this goal for a short- term payout of this length.

The U.S. Geological Survey and Minerals Management Service estimates unproven potential U.S. reserves at 179 billion barrels. Much of this oil is on federal land and offshore areas that are closed to exploration and drilling under congressional moratoriums and presidential executive orders. Few data exist for areas now closed to drilling. Federal agencies and oil companies are prevented from carrying out geological surveys in the areas under drilling moratoriums. The last seismic imagery in several areas of interest was in the 1970's when this technology was more primitive.[3]

Continental U.S.	19 Billion Barrels
Gulf of Mexico	86
Alaska	50
Pacific	14
Atlantic	10
Total	**179**

Based on these data, known and potential petroleum reserves in the U.S. could sustain 14 million barrels per day level of production for thirty-five years and give us time to develop alternative fuels and infrastructure to lessen the need for massive amounts of crude oil.

Why do we need to increase U.S. domestic oil production to 14 million barrels per day?

World production is currently 86 million barrels per day with little room for increase in the short-term. World consumption is increasing at the rate of 2%

---

[2] 2005 Annual Report, DOE/EIA-0216(2005) (November 2006).
[3] R. Gold, B. Casselman, S. Power, "Oil Industry, Lawmakers Aim to Lift Bans on Drilling," *The Wall Street Journal*, May 23, 2008.

to 3% per year. Setting the goal of increasing domestic production and making even limited progress toward that goal will have an immediate effect on oil prices and availability.

Arguments against drilling are that a few million barrels per day will not make us energy independent, and it will be years before we can produce significantly more oil. Those arguments miss the point entirely. Every additional barrel of oil we produce daily subtracts from the amount we have to import from foreign sources. That, in turn, reduces our foreign trade deficit and devaluation of the dollar.

The reason for drilling is not to expand our energy use or reduce fuel prices; it is to stop the drain on the dollar!

Increased oil production will buy us time for longer-range solutions. If we do not pursue this in the short-run, we will be in far worse position by the time longer-term alternative fuel solutions are developed.

IMMEDIATE ACTION – KNOWN RESERVES

Arctic National Wildlife Reserve (ANWR)

Development of ANWR will produce one to two million barrels per day. Infrastructure will have to be constructed to support drilling and production of this field, including a pipeline to the southern coast of Alaska. An argument against drilling in ANWR is that it will only produce one to two million barrels per day. This is 25% of the 7 million barrels per day we need to help us attain energy independence. One million barrels per day of oil at $120 per barrel costs $43.8 billion per year. ANWR will reduce our trade deficit by as much as $88 billion per year.

Fields on the Arctic Shelf

Prudhoe Bay and the Arctic Shelf will increase production an additional one to two million barrels per day. Oil from both of the projects can be transported through the same pipelines. The technology to construct environmentally safe pipelines that will not pollute or melt the tundra is known. These two projects will be one-third to one-half of our goal.

Offshore California and Florida

Laws remain in effect preventing U.S. companies from drilling in these areas. There are reports that Cuba and China have negotiated to explore the Gulf for potential drilling sites in areas bordering Floridian waters. Congressional leadership has refused to bring this to a vote. Prohibition of exploring and drilling in these waters must be reconsidered.

Tertiary Recovery and Stimulation of Old Wells

There is still a large amount of oil in reserves of nominally depleted wells. Many of these formations can be stimulated for further production.

Each of these goals will take a few years to develop. However, it appears reasonable to estimate U.S. production can be increased by as much as 5 million barrels per day within five years.

INTERMEDIATE ACTION – PROBABLE RESERVES

Explore and Drill in the Continental United States

This includes drilling in new fields in North Dakota and known fields on federal land. All of these actions can be ongoing with the immediate goals discussed above.

Increase Deep Water Drilling

Use new technology to drill in deeper waters (>10,000 ft.) further offshore in the Gulf of Mexico. New technology is environmentally safe. During Hurricane Katrina, many drilling platforms were hit and there were no substantial oil spills.

The combination of these actions will bring us an additional 7 millions barrels per day by 2020 giving us time to develop alternative fuels to replace petroleum fuels.

How will decades-old moratoriums on oil production be overturned?

Massive resistance has built up in the U.S. by environmentalists who oppose any effort to increase oil production, build new refineries, and construct coal and nuclear power plants. Environmentalists can bring enormous pressure to bear at the highest levels of government. While this author agrees that we must respect the environment and preserve the earth for future generations, we must also look at safe methods of extracting energy and meeting the needs of our country and population.

If we do not move toward energy independence, devaluation of the dollar will bring unaffordable energy costs resulting in a meltdown of the U.S. economy. At that point, desperation to secure domestic sources of oil will lead to 'quick fix' actions that could be far more environmentally unfriendly than a well thought out plan where all concerns are considered. Since world economies are so globally tied, a disruption in the U.S. economy could cause worldwide turmoil including the possibility of military action to secure vital resources.

The answer is for the U.S. to become energy independent by exploring and producing oil and other energy sources in environmentally safe ways. U.S. oil companies can contribute solutions to environmental issues by improving their drilling operations and production technology. The Federal Environmental Protection Agency can be used to monitor activity and assure that safe procedures are used. This makes far more sense asking foreign governments focused solely on output to supply our energy.

From recorded data, we know that scientists have measured the level of carbon dioxide in our atmosphere since the eighteenth century. Comparative results reveal that the level of carbon dioxide has increased from 280 parts per million (ppm) in 1750 to 370 ppm in 2000 with most of that change since 1950.[4] The proposals presented in this book for attaining U.S. energy independence by 2020 will significantly reduce the production of carbon dioxide from U.S. sources.[5] This will be possible by the decreasing use of hydrocarbon fuels and replacing coal with nuclear energy for the generation of electricity. The end result will promote harmony with the environment.

SUMMARY

The United States is capable of increasing production that will alleviate a substantial portion of our immediate needs as long-term plans are structured for the future. This will require sacrifice and compromise, and elicit

---

[4] Greenhouse gases, Climate Change and Energy, www.eia.doe.gov/oiaf/1605/ggcebro/chapter1.html.
[5] Appendix G.

cooperation between environmentalists, government and the oil industry. Presidential leadership will be required to develop and effectively communicate solid energy policies to educate our citizenry.

Chapter 3

Reducing Petroleum-Based Fuel Consumption in the U.S.

Goal #2. Decrease U.S. Petroleum Consumption by 20% with Conservation, Alternative Fuels, Fuel Additives and Engineering.

The second interim goal is to reduce our consumption of petroleum fluids by 20%. Increasing U.S. production by 100% from 7 to 14 million barrels per day and decreasing consumption to 17 million barrels per day will reduce the amount of crude oil we currently import by 11 million barrels per day. These actions will shrink our balance of payments deficit and help stabilize the dollar. This interim goal is part of our long-term plan to replace all petroleum products from foreign oil sources with domestically produced crude oil and alternative fuels.

Once again, focused leadership is the key to guide the U.S. on this formidable journey. We are a country 'spoiled' by our ability to travel when and where we choose and have every type of consumer product at our disposal. **We have learned to recycle, and we can learn to conserve our limited petroleum resources.**

We must first understand our usage of petroleum. For every barrel of crude oil consumed, 74.7% of that barrel is used in transportation. The breakdown of oil use in transportation modes[1] is as follows:

> Automobiles and Light Trucks – 44.2% as Gasoline
> Commercial Trucks and Buses - 13.8% as Low Emission Diesel Fuel
> Aviation - 7.7% as Heavier Distillate Fuel
> Water – 3.4% as Distillate Fuel and Residual Oil
> Railroads – 1.5% as Off-Road Diesel Fuel
> Military and Miscellaneous – 4.1%

Steps to Reduce the Consumption of Petroleum-Based Fuels

This chapter will review the following topics in each transportation category:

---

[1] Appendix D.

- Fuel Efficiency
- Alternative Modes of Transportation
- Alternative Fuels
- Public Awareness and Support

AUTOMOBILES AND LIGHT TRUCKS

Logically, step one is to tackle our petroleum consumption by automobiles and light trucks. By far, this sector of transportation devours the most petroleum. The good news is that there are many ways to reduce fuel consumption in automobiles and light trucks. A one-third reduction of petroleum-based fuel in this sector would reduce U.S. consumption by fourteen percent or 3 million barrels per day.

The number of automobiles and light trucks in the U.S. has more than tripled since 1970 and the number of drivers has increased at a faster pace than the population. Figure 5 illustrates these growth rates[2]. The increase in volume of vehicles explains the escalation in petroleum-based fuel consumption in this sector. To achieve a one-third reduction in consumption in this area, fuel efficiency must improve and the number of miles driven must decrease. Both of these are possible.

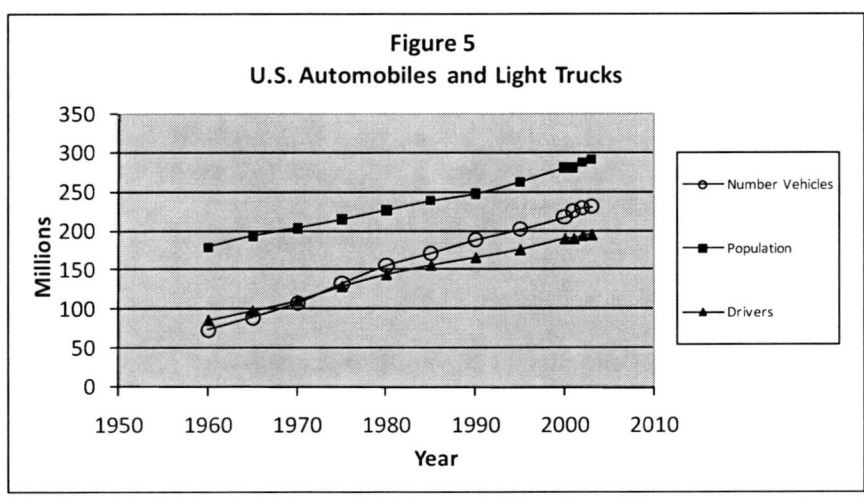

---

[2] U.S. Department of Transportation, Energy Information Agency.

Fuel Efficiency

Currently, automobiles and light trucks average about 17 mpg. There has not been a significant improvement in fuel efficiency since 1990, and there are few cars with better than 25 mpg consumption – see Figure 6.[3] Changing the consumption rate of these types of vehicles is an enormous task. . Current regulations require new vehicle fleets to attain 35 mpg beginning in 2020. But even the most stringent mandated fuel economy regulations for manufacturers in 2020 will not affect our vehicle population as a whole. In 2006, the median age of automobiles and light trucks in the U.S. was 9.2 and 6.8 years respectively. Thus, it will be well beyond 2020 - as vehicles are retired and replaced - before the majority of vehicles on our roads register 35 mpg. We don't have the luxury to delay the inevitable, and we must tighten our belts!

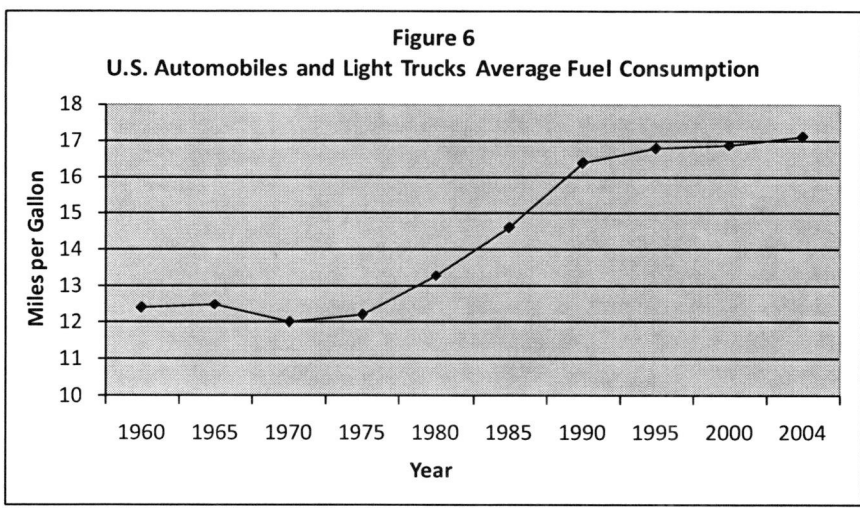

Figure 6
U.S. Automobiles and Light Trucks Average Fuel Consumption

CAFE Standards[4]

Proposal: Set a CAFE Standard of a 35 mpg Fleet Average for New Automobiles and Light Trucks Sold in the U.S. by 2012. This is a radical change from our current legislation. The automobile industry will be faced with a tremendous challenge – a challenge that will reward innovation and creativity. Major design modifications and retooling will be required to meet this

---

[3] U.S. Department of Transportation. www.usdot.gov.
[4] Corporate Average Fuel Economy. This is the average fuel economy of all automobiles and trucks manufactured by a single manufacturer in one year.

ambitious goal. Under this proposal, assuming normal turnover of automobiles and light trucks; 50% of our total fleet would be at 35 mpg by 2020.

Incentives for early retirement of low mileage vehicles can be offered to owners and manufacturers. Tax incentives can also be used to help the U.S. automotive industry cover losses during this change over period. Dangle substantial financial rewards to the American public to help solve some of our challenges, and entrepreneurs of all ages will be burning the midnight oil or, more likely electricity, finding solutions!

Achieving this standard will require weight reduction and smaller engines. This will, in effect, eliminate large light-duty trucks and SUV's. Aviation technology is available for low weight composite materials to reduce vehicle weight without commensurate volume reduction.

Both General Motors and Ford currently manufacture high quality fuel-efficient vehicles in Europe. [5,6] For various reasons, these vehicles have never been introduced into the U.S. Toyota, Nissan, Honda, Mazda, Chrysler and other companies manufacture similar fuel-efficient cars and small trucks worldwide. In 2007, there were only two models sold in the U.S. that had gas mileage of 40 mpg or higher – the Honda Civic Hybrid and the Toyota Prius hybrid. Overseas and mostly in Europe, there are 113 vehicles with 40 mpg performance or higher, up from 86 models in 2005. To further add insult to injury, approximately two-thirds of the 113 high mileage models are made by U.S. based manufacturers or foreign manufacturers that have substantial U.S. sales. It is further pointed out that these cars meet or exceed U.S. safety standards.

The usual excuses about union contracts and American buying habits are not acceptable. If American car and truck manufacturers continue building high fuel consumption vehicles, the companies will disappear and auto workers will lose their jobs. At the same time, the American public must take responsibility for its appetite for large, heavy fuel inefficient vehicles and change its habits.

Hybrid Vehicles

Vehicles with combination gasoline and electric power drive systems are available in limited numbers. This technology has struggled with several

---

[5] "U.S. 'stuck in reverse' on fuel economy", Roland Jones, MSNBC, updated Feb. 28, 2007, www.cleanmpg.com/forums/showthread.php?t=3631
[6] "Fuel economy in automobiles", Wikipedia, http://en.wikipedia.org/wiki?fuel_economy_in_automobiles.

problems. Batteries are costly to manufacture in terms of raw materials and energy. Battery disposal raises environmental concerns. Current economics based on fuel consumption do not justify the cost and maintenance of these vehicles. Finding solutions to overcome these drawbacks, and improvement in electricity storage technology will stimulate the market for hybrid vehicles.

Electric Cars and Trucks

Both hybrid and electric vehicles will benefit from research and development on electricity storage. [7] Electric cars are currently used in relatively short-range travel such as commuting. The practical range for an electric vehicle is 100 miles with a three-hour charging time. Development of an affordable battery-powered vehicle with a 200-mile range would be a significant breakthrough. The recharging time of batteries is a definite handicap for extended travel. A 'wish list' would include the capability of these batteries to be recharged in the approximate time required to fill a gasoline tank. The consumer market is waiting for the technology to advance.

Fuel Additives

Fuel additives are another method of achieving small but significant reduction in fuel consumption. Combustion catalyst technology is now available that reduces fuel consumption by 6% in Diesel engines operating on low emission Diesel fuel.[8,9] Fuel additives can yield improved engine performance - enhancing efficient operation. Fuel additives are discussed in more detail in Appendix E.

Alternative Modes of Transportation

Everyone should consider replacing routine or local automobile travel with more efficient modes of transportation. Expansion and utilization of current transportation options and concepts would yield immediate benefits. Some transportation systems will require building the necessary infrastructure and are therefore considered long-term in nature.

---

[7] "Electric Car", MSN Encarta Encyclopedia, http://encarta.msn.com/text_761580732___0/Electric_Car.html
[8] SFA International, Inc., web site, www.sfainternational.com.
[9] May, Walter R., "Hydrocarbon Fuel Chemistry: Effects of Sulfur on Combustion Reaction Rates," Paper No. 1207537, American Chemical Society, Division of Fuel Chemistry, Philadelphia, PA, August, 2008.

Public Transportation

Bus transportation provides communities with substantial fuel efficiencies. A vehicle with one occupant consumes one gallon per 17 miles. A 5-mpg bus carrying 40 passengers consumes 4 gallons in 20 miles providing more than ten times the fuel efficiency per passenger. Houston, TX has centers where drivers can park their cars in suburban areas and take express buses to their destination. Freeways have express lanes for buses and multi-passenger vehicles.

In the early-twentieth century, many cities had streetcars or trolleys that operated on electricity from overhead wires. Unfortunately, usage waned in the mid-twentieth century. This type of transportation is still relied upon in many countries, and there has been a recent resurrection of 'Modern Streetcars' to improve public transportation in the some U.S. cities.[10] The development of new light rail systems has also been a focus of many municipalities in recent years. Streetcars mix with road traffic whereas light rail often has dedicated rights-of-way and off-street travel. Arguments have been heated over the cost, routes, and alternatives to light rail. As the cost of petroleum fuels escalate, the advantages of light rail increase from use of electricity rather than liquid fuels. Light rail also eliminates the pollution from Diesel powered buses. To reduce our petroleum usage, cities need to seriously review the expansion or construction of electric powered transportation systems as this technology will become a necessary part of our future transportation systems.

Van and Car Pool Programs

Incentives are needed to promote company programs for transporting larger numbers of people at about the same fuel consumption as a single SUV. Coupled with this, municipalities that have not initiated car pool programs should also be encouraged to combine passengers in private automobiles.

Longer and Fewer Work Days and Work-At-Home Solutions

Companies should also consider programs to work 80 hours in nine days yielding a 10% reduction in commuting to work. With computers, the Internet and broadband communications, work-at-home can be as effective in many cases as working in an office. An alternative is to travel to the office for meetings and conferences only when necessary.

---

[10] "Bringing Transit to the City Center", www.tucsontransitstudy.com.

Alternative Fuels

There are few alternative fuels for automobiles and light trucks at the present time. The use of ethanol in gasoline was a 'quick fix' step, but flawed. The production of ethanol consumes more petroleum-based fuel than it replaces. There is also the issue of using food sources for fuel. Use is limited to spark-ignited engines (gasoline).

Bio-Diesel is a step in the right direction. Bio-Diesel is made from materials that might be disposed otherwise (cooking oil, etc.). It can also be made from plants that do not have human food value. The negatives are limitations on supply and lower heat value than petroleum-based fuels. It is limited to use in compression-ignited (Diesel) engines.

Natural gas is a possibility for light trucks and automobiles that travel in areas where the fuel is available.[11] Conversion to LNG use requires engine modification for a gaseous fuel and installation of special tanks. Few if any new light trucks and cars are equipped for gaseous fuel use at the present time. Flex-fuel use is not a possibility between gaseous and liquid fuels.

Public Awareness and Support

The increase in fuel prices has caused serious rethinking of consumption and priorities. There are no smiling faces at the gas pumps – especially when we remember the cost of a full tank just a year ago – and justifiably worry about future prices. We now have some sympathy for those 'across the pond,' and realize we have magically escaped the reality of finite petroleum reserves. This reality is a boulder on the road, and we no longer can postpone a plan to deal with our energy future.

Allow Gasoline Prices to be Market Based

Accounting for inflation adjusted dollars, $4.00+/gallon is the highest real cost in our history. The current pricing has created conservation change. Only when the public feels the full force of the devalued dollar and the inflated cost of oil will consumer 'habits' be modified. Reducing taxes and 'quick fix' therapy to reduce the cost of gasoline and Diesel fuel only delays the obvious.

---

[11] Appendix F.

Education and Curbing Opposition

Whenever light rail or street car construction is proposed, there is inevitable opposition. Protests come from individuals and local neighborhood groups and also organizations and politicians at the national level. Most of the opposition is based around NIMBY[12], neighborhood protection, aggravation, and business dislocation or loss of business during construction. Concerns are valid and change is not always easy. Our society must 'gift' the future. We are enjoying many benefits that our ancestors sacrificed for us. We must continue their foresight.

We need discussion of the advantages of alternative transportation modes to reduce petroleum-based fuel consumption, automobile and light truck traffic and pollution from combustion of liquid fuels. The American public is, by and large, reasonable. An accurate presentation of the benefits of light rail and streetcars will win people over to these projects and reduce opposition.

Communicate! Communicate! Communicate!

The American public should receive 'report cards' showing progress toward achieving energy independence goals. Newspapers, magazines, TV and radio all need to regularly convey the statistics on this journey. Reporting should also include correlated data on the U.S. balance of payments and dollar valuation. We need to know with pride that the sacrifices of every household are helping us accomplish our mission. An example of the kind of data that can be reported is given in Appendix E, Table IXa.

We have billboards that count population and other statistics. Signage on freeways that continuously relay the amount and cost of our foreign petroleum imports would help drivers focus on our need to conserve.

COMMERCIAL TRUCKS

Trucks used in hauling freight are the second largest consumer of petroleum fuels using 15.8% of the barrel of crude oil. They present a more difficult task in reducing fuel consumption through conservation.

---

[12] NIMBY – Not in My Back Yard.

Trucks are the dominant carrier of freight in the U.S. as evidenced from the following information[13]:

	Tons Millions		Ton-Miles Billions	
Trucks	10,700	78%	2,639	60%
Rail	2,009	15%	1,239	28%
Water	1,054	8%	539	12%
Air	9	0.1%	9	0.2%
Total	13,772		4,426	

The majority of truck transports are regional; 68% of all tonnage is hauled an average of 133 miles per ton. The portion of freight tonnage hauled by trucks on greater than 500 mile trips is 10% with an average of 1,027 miles per ton. These longer trips are 32% of total ton-miles and more than five times the amount of intermodal freight hauled by railroads. The following points are worth noting:

- Most truck trips are less than 500 miles; trucks do not travel far from their base of operations.
- Truck trips less than 500 miles cannot be replaced by rail since most shippers and customers do not have rail service.
- About one-half of truck fuel is consumed in greater than 500-mile trips representing about one-fifth of total truck trips.
- Replacement of longer truck trips by rail is currently impossible due to lack of capacity.

Fuel Efficiency

The purpose of a truck is to move large weights of freight. A large highway rig weighs approximately 80,000 lbs. or 40 tons and carries 20 tons of freight. New materials technology may lead to some weight reduction thus improving efficiency. This is not a short-term solution to increasing fuel economy.

---

[13] "Transportation: Invest in America, Freight-Rail Bottom Line Report," John Horsley, Executive Director, American Association of State Highway and Transportation Officials, Washington, D.C., 2002. http://www./freight.transportation.org/doc/FreightRailReport.pdf.

Engine Modifications

Truck engine manufacturers such as Cummins, Caterpillar and DDA have made enormous strides in improving emissions and efficiency over the past decade.[14] This has been done through development of computer controls, engine design and cooperation with regulatory agencies in improving fuels.

Multiple Trailer Trucks

One approach to improving efficiency is to pull two or more trailers. Our roads are currently crowded with automobiles, light trucks and other trucks. This is not a safe alternative without dedicated highways.

Fuel Additives

Combustion catalysts are available that reduce fuel consumption in over-the-road trucks operating on low emission Diesel fuel by 6% (see references cited above in the Automobiles and Light Trucks section). Other fuel additives such as Cetane Improvers, lubricity agents, and cleaners improve engine performance and fuel economy. Appendix E elaborates on this subject.

Alternative Modes of Transportation

Because of the volume of truck traffic, speed and service requirements; there are few alternatives. Railroads can provide efficient long-distance movements of containers and trailers where capacity is available. This will be discussed in more detail below in the section on railroads.

Alternative Fuels

Natural gas is the most obvious alternative fuel for commercial trucks in the short-term. This fuel requires engine modifications, and there are distribution challenges. In the beginning, it would be most applicable to trucks that remain close to home base and a fuel source. As supply becomes more widely available, use of the fuel could expand. It seems reasonable to estimate that at least 50% of commercial trucks could be candidates for natural gas fuel in the next few years. That development would reduce petroleum-based fuel consumption by 8%. Tax incentives could jump-start this project.

---

[14] For more information on this, the reader should visit engine manufacturer web sites.

Public Awareness and Support

Trucks are an indispensable part of our transportation network. Every driver of an automobile or light truck is highly aware of the large number of trucks around them in traffic as well as the danger these trucks present to smaller and lighter vehicles. The principle complaints of automobiles and light trucks toward commercial trucks are:

- Size of truck reducing line of sight in traffic
- Pollution and mechanical issues
- Slow acceleration and slower speeds

Because of the sheer numbers and volume of traffic, there are ways to help us live together with less stress. Hauling more trucks across country by rail or construction of new highways such as the Trans Texas Corridor with highways dedicated to trucks will do little to help traffic congestion in metropolitan areas.

These are suggestions whereby our various governments can help truckers save fuel and drive more compatibly with automobiles and lights trucks in congested areas:

- Encourage truck owners to convert vehicles to natural gas where the fuel is available in normal day-to-day activities. Tax rebates or subsidies would be money well spent.
- Where possible, designate lanes on freeways specifically for trucks. Currently, some freeways in Houston have one lane restricted from truck traffic. Restrict the outside lane from automobiles and light trucks except for those vehicles entering or exiting the highway.
- Enforce regulations on pollution. Some trucks emit copious quantities of particulate matter (smoke).
- Alternative modes of transportation for automobiles and light trucks will reduce density of traffic.
- Mandatory driver education emphasizing safety.
- Stricter enforcement of traffic laws.

AVIATION

General aviation consumes 7.3% of the barrel of oil. The U.S. economy depends heavily on aviation for long distance travel. It has generally been fast, convenient and safe although some travelers in recent times may challenge that assumption. The aviation industry involves many people from the construction of airplanes to employment with the airlines and airports. Downsizing this industry will have a major effect on the U.S. economy. Limited downsizing is already in process because of oil prices.

A major problem for commercial aviation is the number of flights. Major flight paths are at saturation levels. Flight delays experienced in 2007 and 2008 were mostly due to the multitude of flights. The smallest perturbation in flight plans echoes through the system resulting in flight delays throughout the country. Most major airports are at or above capacity for take-offs and landings. A reduction of the number of flights would lead to more efficient operation. Airplanes are already approaching full seating as airlines reduce the number of flights.

Fuel Efficiency

Aircraft engine manufacturers, as with truck engine manufacturers, have made strides in improving fuel efficiency and emissions over the past decade. New engines are quieter. New aircraft are larger with less fuel consumption per passenger mile than older planes. While these changes are incremental, any savings is beneficial.

Alternative Modes of Transportation

Air transportation is a vital part of our economy. There is no logical replacement for long distance, fast and convenient air travel. Short trips less than 500 miles can be replaced with high speed rail. This, again, requires major infrastructure changes and is a long-term solution to reducing fuel consumption.

Alternative Fuels

Aircraft require a high energy liquid fuel. Alternative fuels must be similar to petroleum-based fuels in combustion characteristics and heat content. Hydrogen and liquid natural gas are eliminated because of weight of fuel tanks. Ethanol and Bio-Diesel have low heat content. Liquid hydrocarbon fuels synthesized from coal and natural gas can be used in aviation. Chapter 5 provides more detail on these fuels.

Public Awareness and Support

The most logical way to reduce flights is to allow fuel costs to continue to soar. Airlines will have to pass on fuel costs to passengers. Added cost will reduce the number of casual and vacation fliers leading people to evaluate more carefully their reasons for flying. It is unlikely that these effects will reduce the number of flights by as much as 25% in the immediate future, but the long-term effect will be significant. Nevertheless, even a 15% reduction in the use of aviation fuel would reduce 1% of oil consumed.

Another 'out of the box' idea is for airlines to become involved in passenger rail business. This is done in the United Kingdom where some private airline companies operate passenger service on government owned railroads. Continental Airlines is aligned with New Jersey Transit to move people from Manhattan to the Newark airport. Amtrak serves Baltimore Washington International Airport moving people from the airport to neighboring cities. This would preserve jobs and bring new thinking to passenger rail travel.

RAILROADS

Rail transportation, freight and passenger, is part of the short and long-term solution to reducing transportation fuel consumption. Short-term actions are presented here and longer-term goals will be discussed in Chapter 5.

RAILROADS - FREIGHT

Freight railroads carry 28% of total domestic freight in ton-miles including unit trains, carloads and intermodal trains. Intermodal trains carrying 20' and 40' containers and trailers compete with trucks for long distance freight movements. Intermodal freight is 5% of total freight and one-sixth of truck traffic on greater than 500-mile trips.

The majority of major freight lines in the U.S. are near capacity. It is projected that freight tonnage or ton-miles will grow 50% between 2000 and 2020. Studies by the American Association of Railroads[15] report that the level of

---

[15] www.aar.org.

infrastructure investment required for railroads to simply maintain their current share of freight tonnage by 2020 is $215 billion. This investment will come from private companies. This compares with the $1,900 billion planned expenditures by state and federal governments in highways over the same period. Due to fuel savings, it is advantageous to haul freight by rail. In the short-term, railroads will not be able to haul a significantly higher share of freight thus negating the possibility of reducing truck fuel consumption.

Fuel Efficiency

Railroads have a large advantage over trucks in fuel consumption. For the same cost, a train carries a ton of freight 350 miles compared with 100 miles for a truck. This results from railroads having more shallow grades, fewer starts and stops as well as changes in speed and hauling a large number of freight cars in each train.

Engine Design Improvements

Modern freight locomotives for road use are powered by 4,000 hp and larger Diesel engines. These engines are generally two-cycle and have a maximum of 900 rpm compared with four-cycle truck engines with a maximum of 2,100 rpm. Trains generally have multiple engines depending on the tonnage and terrain. In recent years, engine manufacturers have made major improvements in engine design to improve fuel efficiency and reduce emissions. For more information on engines, go to General Electric[16] and EMD[17] web sites.

Fuel Additives

As with trucks, *fuel additives are available that can improve fuel efficiency by 6% and more (see references in the Automobiles and Light Trucks section). Testing is currently underway to expand usage.*[18] Between engine design improvements and fuel additives, the possibility of saving 10% of fuel is achievable with current technology.

---

[16] http://www.ge.com/products_services/rail.html.
[17] http://www.emdiesels.com/lms/emdweb/company/more/060608_repower.html.
[18] See papers on the SFA web site, 'Library' page. www.sfainternational.com.

Alternative Modes of Transportation

Trucks and water (barges) are the alternatives to rail transportation. Water is limited by geography. Trucks cannot carry unit train commodities such as coal at a cost that is comparable with rail. While railroads carry about half the ton-miles of trucks, they are invaluable and irreplaceable where they excel.

Alternative Fuels

Railroad locomotives, like trucks and aircraft, require liquid fuels with high energy content. They are prime candidates for conversion to liquid fuels from coal, natural gas and shale oil. In addition, railroads have the alternative of using electricity as a power source. Most major European rail lines are electrified. The U.S. has few electric railroads with most on the East Coast. Few long distance freight-carrying railroads have operated with electricity in the U.S. other than the Milwaukee and Great Northern Railroads in the northern tier. Both of these were in the first half of the 20th century and were successful at the time. Electricity eliminates petroleum-based fuel consumption.

RAILROADS - COMMUTER AND REGIONAL RAIL SERVICE

Commuter and regional rail must become part of mainstream U.S. lifestyle. Rail lines radiate from and form a network around American cities. Private companies own these rail lines. Seldom-used tracks and abandoned right-of-ways could be used for commuter passenger service. Building tracks for commuter trains that parallel busy freight lines is another possibility to increase capacity. Construction of new tracks and upgrading existing tracks are not short-term propositions. Both are more in the range of mid-term solutions. However, planning should start now to implement increased commuter service. These trains are ideally powered with electricity.

RAILROADS - LONG-DISTANCE PASSENGER SERVICE

We need to expand less than 500-mile long-distance passenger service. In some areas of the country such as between Boston and Washington, Los Angeles and San Diego, and around Chicago and San Francisco, rail passenger service is well developed. Where possible, this service should be improved and enlarged. This can be accomplished through expansion of Amtrak and the use of existing rail lines where capacity makes it possible.

Several states are investing heavily in passenger service. These states include North Carolina, Illinois, Missouri and the upper Midwest. In many instances, major mainlines between cities are already at capacity with freight traffic and are unable to accommodate passenger trains. Expansion of passenger service may not be possible until additional tracks are built. Railroad companies and every level of government will need to cooperate to add and expand passenger service.

Public Awareness and Support

Railroads are the stepchild of the transportation infrastructure in the U.S. Railroad companies are privately owned and operated. There has been a strong resistance to cooperation between government and railroads from both sides. Trucks have offered more flexibility in solving transportation problems. The time has come to work together to use synergistically the strengths of both modes of transportation.

The State of Texas Department of Transportation (TX-DOT) has long held a cavalier attitude toward railroads. In Houston, two rail lines were taken out for freeway construction and expansion in the past five years. While both of these were relatively minor freight lines, they were in active use and would have provided ideal commuter routes.

Amtrak operates on a subsidy from the federal government and is chronically underfunded. Presidential administrations come and go, and all insist that Amtrak must become self-sufficient. There is never consideration of the amount of tax dollars spent on highways, river transportation and aviation. Amtrak will require adequate funding to upgrade facilities and expand its operation.

Amtrak operates regional service between the Baltimore-Washington International airport and cities north and south. The airport train station is served by the Amtrak's New York – Washington mainline. Service is inexpensive, frequent, on time and performs very well. At the same time, the airport train station is seriously in need of maintenance and the train cars, and windows especially, need cleaning - and this is Amtrak's premier route! An effort must be made to educate the public about the contribution of railroads to our economy. Congress must reconsider the role of Amtrak in our transportation system and appropriate the necessary money to adequately fund the operation. This is another area requiring leadership from our elected officials.

INTRACOASTAL AND RIVER TRANSPORTATION

Barges on intra-coastal water ways and rivers haul two-thirds the ton-miles as railroads and consume the same proportional amount of fuel. Engines in tugboats are similar to railroad engines in horsepower and two-cycle operation. These engines consume high energy liquid fuels.

The same comments for alternative fuels in rail use apply to boats with the exception of electricity. Boats are generally fueled at depots. They are ideal candidates for fuel additives that reduce fuel costs and pollution.

MILITARY AND GOVERNMENT

The military duplicates transportation of the country on a smaller scale. It operates a large airline, a major shipping company and a truck line. It also has the equivalent of industrial fuel applications in battlefield equipment. Other government agencies have similar fuel requirements. The government has an advantage in that it can mandate specific fuel use by certain types of vehicles. It has been suggested that all new automobiles and trucks purchased by local and federal governments be equipped to use natural gas. Many government vehicles are fueled at depots making this conversion relatively easy. The government can also mandate use of alternative fuels, more fuel efficient vehicles and other conservation methods such as fuel additives.

SUMMARY

We can significantly reduce petroleum-based fuel consumption in automobiles and light trucks between now and 2020 by conservation, substitution of currently available alternative fuels, expanding alternative modes of transportation, improved engine design and fuel additives. A 33% reduction in this area will reduce crude oil consumption by 15% or 3 million barrels per day.

Conversion of 50% of trucks to natural gas use will lead to a 7% savings in crude oil consumption. That is about 1.5 million barrels per day. Together with the savings in automobiles and light trucks, we will achieve a 20% reduction in crude oil consumption. This will take the pressure off crude oil prices, significantly improve our balance of payments position and give us time to develop alternative fuels to replace petroleum-based fuels.

Chapter 4

Long-Term Energy Sources

Goal #3. Replace All Imported Crude Oil and Petroleum Products with Domestic Production and Alternative Sources of Energy and Fuels.

The United States is the third largest producer of crude oil (2007) in the world after Saudi Arabia and Russia. The U.S. ranks twelfth in proven reserves.[1] Doubling oil production will deplete our proven reserves in less than one decade and estimated unproven reserves within three decades. And, that does not meet our goal of replacing all imports of oil and natural gas. In this chapter, we will discuss sources of energy that can replace oil. Electricity will play a dominant role especially in transportation. This chapter will also cover alternative sources of high energy liquids fuels, low energy liquid fuels and gaseous fuels.

ELECTRICAL ENERGY

Electricity will emerge as an even more critical component of our energy future. The U.S. currently has almost 400 gigawatts of generating capacity. Our capacity may have to expand by as much as 50% to replace petroleum fuel consumption by 2020. The table below illustrates sources of energy for electricity generation in 2007.[2]

Sources of Energy for U.S. Electricity Generation	
Coal	48.00%
Natural Gas	21.50%
Nuclear	19.40%
Hydroelectric	6.00%
Renewable Sources	2.50%
Other	2.60%

Where will the energy come from to generate this additional electricity?

---

[1] Energy Information Administration, January 9, 2007
[2] Appendix F.

Fossil Fuel Energy

Coal

The U.S. has the largest deposits of coal of any nation in the world. In terms of energy, U.S. coal deposits represent 82.6% of the world's petroleum reserves combined.[3] The U.S. burns approximately 100,000 tons of coal per hour with 58% of that used in generating electricity.[4] A negative to use of coal is formation of carbon dioxide in the combustion process - a major concern in global climate change models. The U.S. emits about 60 billion tons of carbon dioxide per year from all sources with 30% derived from coal. Coal exhausts contain mercury, a toxic heavy metal that is now found in seafood and other foods; and thorium, a radioactive element. For these reasons, coal will eventually be eliminated as an energy source for electricity and used for other purposes discussed below.

Natural Gas

The U.S. ranks 2nd in Non-OPEC proven reserves of natural gas[5]**, and yet we are currently importing 16.7% of the natural gas we consume from Canada. There is no excuse for importing any natural gas.** Exploration and production of natural gas must continue as long as our reserves can support it. Natural gas produces about two-thirds of the amount of carbon dioxide produced by coal to generate the same amount of electricity.

Nuclear Energy

Nuclear power is the logical alternative to replace coal and expand electricity generation.[6] The U.S. has a stellar safety record with nuclear power, Three Mile Island included. Nuclear power is used widely in Europe with much higher population density than the U.S. **France generates 75% of its power with nuclear power plants. The U.S. has more nuclear power plants than France although there has been no new construction of power plants since 1970.** Uranium fuel for nuclear power plants is available in the U.S. to meet our needs for decades. Fuel for nuclear power is available for centuries when considering fusion processes.

---

[3] Coal, http://en.wikipedia.org/wiki/coal
[4] This is based on an average heat value of 13,000 Btu's per pound of coal, 2.02 trillion megawatts of electricity generated with coal and 22.7 quadrillion Btu's of energy from coal per year.
[5] Appendix F.
[6] Nuclear Power, Wikipedia, http://en.wikipedia.org/wiki/Nuclear_Power.

Waste Product Disposal

Nuclear power has a significant environmental issue – radioactive byproduct. Without treatment, the residue requires 2,500 years to decay to safe radioactive levels. Technology is available to reduce this radioactivity and recover energy in the process. After treatment, the remaining material requires about 125 years to decay to acceptable radioactive levels. There are safe ways to store this material in remote locations while this decay takes place.

Construction Time

Construction of nuclear power plants is a long-term process. In the past, the time from inception to start-up has been 10 years or longer. Since construction of new nuclear power plants has been halted for the past 30 years, time will be required to train construction workers and reactivate the process. Government assistance in some form will be required since this will be a huge investment and private industry will need incentives to undertake the construction. Large engineering firms such as General Electric and Siemens Westinghouse have the background and engineering knowledge to take on these types of projects. Recent cost estimates for nuclear power plant construction are high and subject to debate.

Nuclear Electricity Costs

Comparison of Electricity Generating Cost by Fuel and Country					
U.S. Cents/kw-hr					
	France 2003	UK 2004	Chicago, U.S. 2004	Canada 2004	Europe 2007
Nuclear	3.7	4.6	4.2 - 4.6	5	5.4 - 7.4
Coal		5.2	3.5 - 4.1	4.5	4.7 - 6.1
Gas	5.8, 10.1	5.9, 9.8	5.5 - 7.0	7.2	4.6 - 6.1
Wind Onshore		7.4			4.7 - 14.8
Wind Offshore		11			8.2 - 20.2

The costs of electricity generated from various modes are given in the table above.[7] These data indicate that nuclear power plants, including capital costs, are within the same range as coal and gas power plants. Carbon credits are not included in these calculations.

---

[7] Appendix F.

Education

Education of the public about nuclear power and its long-term benefits will be required for its acceptance. Unfortunately, man-made mistakes at Chernobyl have caused intense fear. Anxiety generated by the movie "China Syndrome" still echoes through the U.S. twenty-nine years after it was released. Science has provided safeguards. **We cannot allow irrational fears to immobilize our plans to provide energy for future needs. Do we wait until our cities are darkened by power outages before we take action?** Nuclear plants cannot be built overnight and safety concerns require long-term planning.

Nuclear power can expand the generation of electricity and eventually replace coal fired plants thus eliminating carbon dioxide emissions and other pollutants from these plants. It has been pointed out that there is less radioactivity in the environs of a nuclear plant than around a coal plant because of thorium in coal exhausts.

Renewable Energy

Hydroelectric

Electricity generated with waterpower is a renewable resource under stable climatic conditions. Most viable resources of hydroelectric power have been developed in the U.S. As a result, while the quantity of electricity from waterpower has remained constant, the percentage of the total has dropped as total electricity generated has increased.

Wind Farms and Wind Power

Wind power is obviously dependent on the weather. A one megawatt per hour windmill costs $1,000,000 and occupies one acre of land. Larger wind generators produce 2.5 megawatts, are 500 feet tall and occupy 160 acres or one-quarter of a square mile. These generators cost $2.5 million each without considering the cost of the land and connecting grid. Wind farms are not rational sources for large amounts of electricity. The economic investment in wind farms cannot be justified at present day costs to replace large amounts of electricity. There is the problem of base load plants to replace electricity when wind generators underperform. The result is high redundancy in generation capacity.

There are advances in the technology to install low weight rooftop wind turbines on individual structures to generate electricity. Due to design, these small wind turbines have more flexibility to capture wind flow than their large counterparts. Rooftop variances, noise and aesthetics have been a hindrance to their use. In areas that receive adequate wind, the economics may eventually justify the cost.[8]

Solar Energy

Solar power is equally land intensive and more dependent on weather conditions than wind farms. Spain is currently intensifying their effort to capture solar energy by advancing the technology for solar towers.[9] The cost for solar power is similar to wind power.

HIGH ENERGY LIQUID FUELS

Liquid fuels have been the choice for transportation purposes for decades. There are two reasons for this. The first is that the fuel can be stored and transported in light weight tanks without pressurization or temperature control. Fuels in the gas state must be stored in tanks that can withstand the pressure to force the gas into the liquid state or stored at very low temperatures. These tanks must be strong and are heavy.

The second reason is that hydrocarbon liquid fuels contain 18,000 Btu's per pound. A Btu is the energy required to raise the temperature of one pound of water one degree Fahrenheit. To illustrate the energy consumed in transportation, an automobile with 20 mpg fuel efficiency will consume enough energy in 20 miles to raise the temperature of two 55-gallon drums of water from 70° F. to the boiling point.

Liquid Fuels from Petroleum

There will be a demand for liquid fuels for the foreseeable future. Air travel is not possible with the weight of current electrical storage devices or the weight of gaseous fuel tanks. Hybrid vehicles require liquid fuels to supplement and recharge batteries. Oxygenated fuels such as ethanol and Bio-Diesel have less heat value and limits on supply. Ethanol produced for fuel also impacts food supplies. Petroleum fluids will continue to be produced for several decades although there will be an asymptotic drop off as U.S. and world reserves are

---

[8] "Rooftop Wind Turbines Ready for Commercial Use," www.metaefficient.com/renewable-power.
[9] Environment News Service, www.ens-newswire.com/ens/mar2007/2007-03-30-02.asp.

exhausted. There will come a time when petroleum will be more valuable as a raw material for petrochemicals than as a fuel.

We will need high energy level liquid fuels to replace petroleum-based fuels. These fuels must be compatible with petroleum-based fuels so that they are seamlessly interchangeable.[10]

Liquid Fuels from Coal

The technology for producing liquid fuel from coal is well developed. The Fischer-Tropsch and SASOL processes have been known for 100 years. Germany produced large amounts of fuel from coal during World War II. Coal liquids are a major fuel source for South Africa. This process involves hydrogenating and breaking down condensed carbon structures approaching graphite in molecular structure. The Air Force is considering building a plant to convert coal to liquid fuel at its Malmstrom Air Force Base in Montana.[11]

Coal is our most viable source of high energy liquid fuels because of existing technology and known coal reserves.

Liquid Fuels from Natural Gas

High energy liquid fuels similar to petroleum and liquefied coal fuels can be made from natural gas. This involves the opposite process from making liquid fuel from coal. With natural gas, molecules containing one to four carbons are combined into longer chain molecules with five and higher carbon atoms. A modified Fischer-Tropsch or Mobil process can carry out this molecular rearrangement. This process converts the gas to a liquid state at ambient pressure and temperature. Gas-to-Liquid or GTL fuel has been proven in Europe where a ferry ran on liquid fuel from natural gas in 2007. On February 1, 2008, an Airbus A380 was the first airplane to fly with GTL-based fuel. U.S. natural gas reserves make this source of energy a second viable option.[12]

The processes for converting coal and natural gas into liquid fuels require energy input and water; and produce carbon dioxide and waste. Research and development is needed to improve the technology and efficiency of these processes.

---

[10] Appendix E.
[11] "Air Force turning to coal for cleaner-burning fuel", M. Brown, Houston Chronicle, March 22, 2008.
[12] "Gas to Liquids," http://en.wikipedia.org/wiki/Gas_to_Liquids

Shale Oil

The U.S. has plentiful deposits of shale oil.[13] These sources approach world petroleum reserves in comparable energy value. Producing hydrocarbon fuels from shale oil is difficult and has never developed into a viable commercial source of energy. Shell Oil Company has made a large commitment to developing hydrocarbon fuels from shale oil.

Tar Sands

Tar sands have been developed in Alberta, Canada as a source of petroleum fuel. There are severe environmental impacts in producing this energy. The negative is that the U.S. does not have large-scale domestic deposits of this material.

LOW ENERGY LIQUID FUELS

Bio-Diesel

Bio-Diesel will remain in use if for no other reason than it is an environmentally friendly method of using materials that must otherwise be disposed of such as cooking oils. Bio-Diesel, an oxygenated fuel, has a heat content of about 17,000 Btu's per pound compared with Diesel fuel at 18,700 Btu's per pound. It can be mixed with hydrocarbon fuels and used effectively in Diesel engines.

Ethanol

Ethanol is not, in the opinion of this author, a rational choice for a liquid fuel. The cost and energy to produce it is on the same order of magnitude as the fuel it replaces. It is an oxygenated fuel with lower heat value than hydrocarbon fuels, about 11,000 Btu's per pound. Ethanol made from corn diverts food to fuel use. This has caused major inflation in food costs around the world. **Ethanol is a bad idea that should be abandoned.**

---

[13] Appendix E.

GASEOUS FUELS

Fuels in the gas state have the advantage of very clean combustion with reduced or, in the case of hydrogen, no pollution. Natural gas produces about two-thirds the weight of carbon dioxide as liquids fuels and coal for the same amount of energy.[14] The disadvantages are distributing and storing these fuels. They require heavy tanks capable of holding the fuel under pressure. This effectively rules out use in airplanes.

Natural Gas

Natural gas was discussed in Chapter 3 as one of the alternative fuels currently available.[15]

Hydrogen

Hydrogen is a totally clean burning fuel. The only byproduct of combustion is water. However, hydrogen fuel is the classic example of the statement "There is no such thing as a free lunch." Hydrogen is not naturally occurring. It is made by electrolysis of water, a chemical process whereby water is converted into hydrogen and oxygen with electricity. With plentiful nuclear power, hydrogen could become a significant fuel in future transportation. Engines can be designed for dual or multiple fuel use including hydrogen as one of the fuels.

The infrastructure to manufacture and distribute hydrogen on a level to significantly impact transportation uses does not currently exist. This will require building plants and increasing electricity generation as discussed above. Requiring use of hydrogen in government owned vehicles where it is practical will help jump start this industry.

SUMMARY

Alternative fuels are the key to ultimately replacing fourteen million barrels per day of oil in our transportation system. The technology exists to replace foreign oil and diminishing supplies of domestic oil with alternative fuels.

---

[14] Appendix G.
[15] Appendix F.

The U.S. has 17 million barrels per day refining capacity. With oil consumption reduced, excess refining capacity can be converted to producing liquid or gaseous fuels from these alternative sources. Additional research and development will be necessary. The government can support this with tax write-offs and grants. It is this author's opinion that liquid fuels from coal and natural gas will be the primary replacement for petroleum liquid fuels as petroleum reserves are exhausted.

Nuclear power plants can meet future requirements and eventually replace existing coal plants although the latter will be decades in the future. Coal and natural gas may become too valuable as replacements for liquid petroleum fuels to consume these fuel resources to generate electricity.

The U.S. has sufficient energy sources to meet its requirements through the 21st century while maintaining energy independence. This does not remove the need to permanently reduce consumption of petroleum-based liquid fuel for transportation commensurate with available sources as discussed in Chapters 3 and 5. We must use our energy wisely - not wastefully.

Chapter 5

Long-Term Solutions to Reduce Energy Consumption

Goal #4. Rebuild our Transportation Infrastructure to Use Different Sources of Energy that Permanently Replace Petroleum Based Fuels.

Reaching and maintaining energy independence in the U.S. requires major restructuring of transportation to allow use of alternative fuels. Petroleum provides 40% of our total energy consumption and 70.6% of the barrel is devoted to transportation not including military uses. Mathematically, we calculate that transportation absorbs 28% of our total demand for energy. With few exceptions, we are totally dependent on petroleum to meet our transportation needs. In this chapter, we will examine all modes of transportation and consider viable ways to replace current petroleum-based fuels with alternative fuels and at the same time maintain our economy and freedom to move[1].

There are some who say that world petroleum production has peaked. Others believe that time may be a decade or more in the future. In either case, petroleum is a finite commodity. While petroleum will remain a source for fuels for several decades, sooner or later alternative fuels will have to be substituted for petroleum-based fuels. Moving toward alternative fuels now will allow flexibility and adequate time to develop a plan of action for us and future generations.

AUTOMOBILES AND LIGHT TRUCKS

Of all modes of transportation, automobiles and light trucks are most adaptable to alternative fuels and some degree of flex-fuel capability. Ideally, a futuristic vehicle should use most or all available fuels. This could result in a significant shift from spark-ignited (gasoline) to more fuel flexible compression-ignited (Diesel) engines.

---

[1] Appendix H.

Liquid Fuels

As indicated in Chapter 4, liquid fuels can come from a variety of sources. These include high energy fuels from oil, shale oil, tar sands, coal and natural gas. They also include low energy fuels from Bio-Diesel and ethanol. Future vehicles must have flex-fuel capability for seamless interchangeability of all liquid fuels.

Gaseous Fuels

There are two gaseous fuels that can be used in automobiles and light trucks; liquid natural gas (LNG or CNG) and hydrogen. Operating a reciprocating engine on gaseous fuels requires a fuel handling system that is different from liquid fuels. There are few new vehicles equipped for gaseous fuel use at the present time. Engine modifications would require pressurized fuel tanks and special equipment from the tank to the engine manifold. Flex-fuel capability between gaseous and liquid fuels does not appear to be an option.

Service stations providing gaseous fuels will have to develop a different business model for distribution of liquid fuels. Separate storage tanks for the fuel will be required. Filling a fuel tank with gaseous fuels is more complicated and inherently more dangerous than filling a tank with liquid fuel. Trained personnel will be required for this. These issues must be resolved to expand use of liquid fuels. As indicated in Chapter 3, the most likely initial users of gaseous fuels will be those that fuel their tanks at depots such as trucks. Development of a wide network of service stations dispensing gaseous fuels will take time.

A serious proposal has been made that government owned vehicles be required to use gaseous fuels. As with trucks, they can be filled at depots or garages. This would speed the acceptance of gas fuels and expand development of the distribution system.

Electricity

Electricity Storage

The fundamental problem with electric vehicles is the battery. Electricity storage devices – mostly known as batteries – have several problems.

- They store a relatively small amount of energy compared to a liquid or gas fuel tank. This results in short ranges for electric vehicles.

- They are expensive to manufacture.
- Recharging is a long process – three hours or more.
- Manufacturing and disposal costs are greater than the petroleum-based fuels that they avoid consuming.
- Batteries have environmental impact in disposal. Batteries contain metals and other chemicals that can become an environmental concern.

Battery Operated Electric Cars

Electric cars powered solely by batteries are not practical, even for short-range trips. The range is 100 miles which is a 50 mile round trip. Because of the limited energy available, size and weight carrying capability are critical issues. This is not a feasible alternative until improvements are made in electricity storage.

Hybrid Technology

Hybrid technology offers the best of electric car advantages and minimizes the disadvantages of gasoline cars. The battery allows the engine to shut down when the car is stopped. The car starts on battery power and shifts over to gasoline power when car speed or battery charge requires it. The hybrid has the same battery disadvantages described above.

Fuel Cells

Although the technology is not well developed, power from fuel cells may offer more promise than batteries. Fuel cells produce electricity from chemical reaction. At this time, power output and cost have not become practical.[2]

COMMERCIAL TRUCKS

The options for commercial trucks are more limited than automobiles and light trucks because of the difference in weight and energy requirements.

---

[2] Fuel Cells, http://en.wikipedia.org/wiki/Fuel_Cell

Liquid Fuels

Liquid fuels from petroleum and alternative sources are expected to be totally interchangeable in truck engines. Large truck engines are compression-ignited. This eliminates use of alcohols. Bio-Diesel can be substituted in these engines.

Gaseous Fuels

Liquid Natural Gas (LNG)

LNG was proposed in Chapter 3 as an immediate alternative fuel for trucks that stay close to locations that dispense gas. This is a good option that will eliminate petroleum fuel use. With wider availability at truck stops, LNG can become a significant fuel for commercial trucks in the immediate future.

Hydrogen

Hydrogen could become an alternative fuel for trucks, especially if a truck engine can be adapted to use both LNG and hydrogen. Hydrogen has the advantage that no carbon dioxide is produced in the combustion process.

Electricity

Batteries are not powerful enough for trucks except in limited application. There is a futuristic proposal for electric powered trucks in the Trans-Texas Corridor section later in this chapter.

RAILROADS

Railroads were the transportation system that bound together the United States from coast to coast. Railroad construction began in 1830 and became one of the deciding factors in the outcome of the War Between the States. The north had a much better rail network than the south. Before rail, the time to travel overland from the east coast to the west coast was about one year or 8,000 hours. By 1900, that travel time was reduced to 80 hours, a 100-fold reduction. In comparison, jet aircraft reduced that travel time to about 8 hours, a 10-fold reduction. Railroads had an enormous impact on the U.S. through World War II.

Railroad tracks grew to about 220,000 miles by 1920. With the advent of automobiles and trucks, rail use decreased. Many lines with little or no traffic to support maintenance and taxes were dismantled. The current amount of tracks in the U.S. is 140,490 miles[3].

There was once a large rail passenger network in the U.S. With the National Highway Defense Act and construction of the Interstate road system beginning in the 1950's, passenger rail decayed and was adsorbed into Amtrak in 1969. Except for California, the area around Chicago and the Boston to Washington corridor, passenger service is almost nonexistent in the U.S. Long-distance Amtrak trains are more like cruise ships than serious passenger conveyance.

Railroads hit a nadir in the 1970's. Since then, freight ton-miles have increased significantly. Rail lines that were downgraded or taken out have been rebuilt. Railroads have a distinct disadvantage over trucks and commercial aviation in that maintenance and expansion must be paid out of earnings whereas tax money is used for highways, airports and air traffic control.

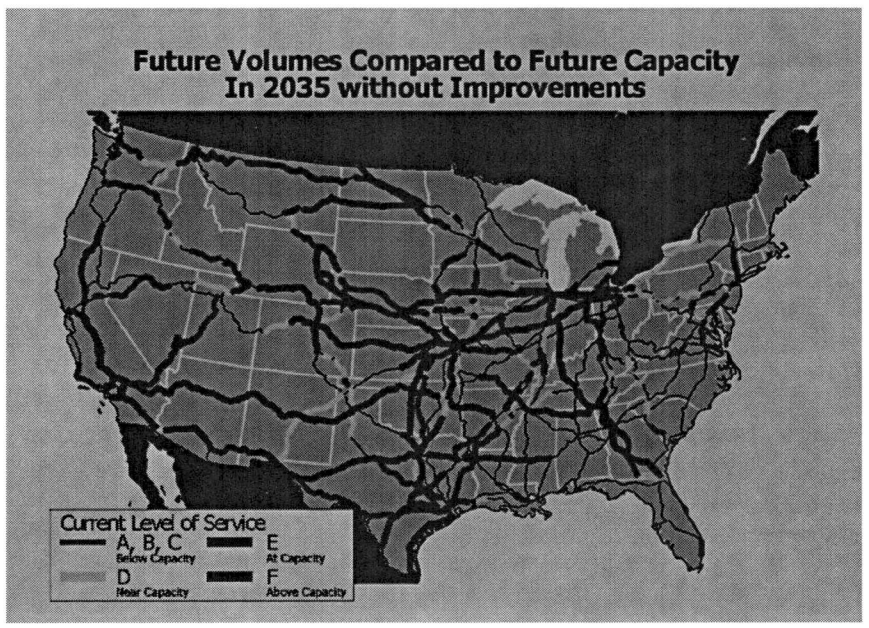

---

[3] American Association of Railroads, www.aar.com.

The American Association of Railroads has done a study of major rail lines that are at or near capacity. The map above delineates only principle freight mainlines. If planned maintenance and upgrading are not done, many lines will be at or above capacity based on current projections. This projection does not consider the effect of adding a large number of trains hauling trucks in intermodal service to the existing system. Planned upgrades include adding double and multiple tracks in some areas, expanding centralized traffic control, reducing highway grade crossings and improving classification yards. Upgrades do not appear to include electrification.

Liquid Fuels

The same comments for liquid fuels related to commercial trucks apply to railroad locomotives. As discussed in Chapter 3, railroad engines are much larger than truck engines and more like domestic waterway vessels. High energy liquid fuels or blends with small amounts of Bio-Diesel are required for all these engines.

Gaseous Fuels

The use of gaseous fuels in railroad locomotive engines has the same advantages as in trucks. Practical considerations do not weigh in favor of its use in the railroad setting. Fitting a gaseous fuel tank under a locomotive could present significant engineering problems. There is also the distribution problem since railroad locomotives do not fill up at service stations or truck stops. Safety would also be a consideration. A locomotive typically carries 1,500 gallons or more fuel. A similar amount of gaseous fuel would be an extreme danger in an accident situation.

Electricity

Because a railroad locomotive operates on a track with very limited lateral motion, they can take power from an overhead catenary with a pantograph on the top of the engine and operate purely on electricity.

The U.S. has limited lines equipped with electrical power compared with Europe where electrical power is widely used. Electric power requires high-density traffic. The use of electrical power will result in a much cleaner operation and reduce pollution. The cost to electrify a rail line approaches the cost to construct a new railroad.

Electric power can come from nuclear power plants completely eliminating production of carbon dioxide. Upgrading high traffic density rail lines to double and triple tracks, as well as construction of new lines, should include electrification in the project.

High Speed Passenger Railroads

Reducing automobile and light truck fuel consumption by 33% and replacing air travel for flights up to 500 miles will require building a high speed passenger rail network. Europe, Japan and Korea have networks in place. These trains travel at 300 Kilometers per hour (180 mph). At that speed, the time from one city center to another 300 miles away will be equal to or faster than air. For example, flights between London and Paris have been eliminated except for a few connecting flights. More importantly, trains can run on electricity generated by nuclear power plants. This will replace a significant sector of transportation with non-petroleum fuel.

High speed rail is not compatible with slower freight trains. Therefore, separate tracks will have to be built for high speed passenger trains although they can parallel current rail lines in some instances. Some trains can be designed to haul cars and small light trucks belonging to passengers. This will give passengers the flexibility of low cost, high speed travel plus having their automobiles at the destination.

High speed rail can potentially save 25% of the fuel currently used by aviation.

THE TRANS-TEXAS CORRIDOR

One of the more innovative ideas for transportation is the Trans-Texas Corridor. Introduced in January 2002, the Trans-Texas Corridor calls for a 4,000 mile system within Texas that incorporates toll and non-toll roads, high speed freight and commuter rail, water lines, oil and gas pipelines, electric transmission lines, broadband and other telecommunications infrastructures in the corridor. These corridors would be up to a quarter mile wide in places to accommodate all this activity. They would pass through 143 of the state's 254 counties and are projected to cost between $145 and $185 billion dollars. Financing is expected to come from private sources.

The plan includes separate highway lanes for passenger vehicles (three in each direction) and trucks (two lanes in each direction). There would be six rail lines, two for high speed passenger trains, two for commuter or regional trains and two for freight. Since there would be no automobiles in the truck lanes, the option would be available for tractors to pull several trailers for much better fuel consumption per ton-mile of freight hauled.

This concept, while garnering considerable opposition from groups such as the Farm Bureau, would alleviate several transportation issues and make a substantial move toward reducing petroleum fuel consumption and replacing it with electricity. All the rail lines can be electrified. It also makes possible innovative new concepts for moving trucks with electricity.

Consider this 'out of the box' idea. Technology is available to replace truck transmissions with electric generators and power the wheels with traction motors similar to railroad locomotives. With this type of power transmission, a truck could move from customer or terminal to the corridor where it would enter a truck lane. A pantograph on top of the tractor would be raised to make contact with the catenary or electric wire system overhead. Technology exists to take control of the steering and speed with computer controls to operate the truck independent of the driver. The Diesel engine would be shut down and all power would come from the catenary. The truck would be protected by radar to prevent collisions with trucks stopped in the lane. Steering could be controlled from the roadway to keep the truck aligned with the catenary.

Freight tonnage projections for 2020 and beyond indicate a growth of the economy at a far greater rate than can be sustained with the most aggressive investment in the existing rail system. Therefore, while movement of intermodal freight will grow substantially, especially for very long distances, there is no expectation that the current six to one ratio of long distance (greater than 1,000 mile) truck freight movements to rail intermodal freight will change significantly even with substantial investment in the current rail network. The Trans-Texas Corridor concept will bring new rail lines and highways that will not only relieve congestion, it is also possible to change the source of power from petroleum or high energy liquid fuels to electricity. This will also reduce the production of carbon dioxide.

INTRACOASTAL AND RIVER TRANSPORTATION

The same comments for alternative fuels in rail use apply to boats excepting for electricity. Boats are generally fueled at depots. They are ideal candidates for fuel additives that produce fuel savings and reduce pollution.

AVIATION

Aviation consumes 7.7% of our total petroleum consumption. Take-off burns the largest amount of fuel. Ascent is controlled by the physics of accelerating as much as 400 tons of mass to 500 mph or more and lifting that mass 7 miles above the ground. A fully loaded Boeing 747 in Chicago bound for Tokyo weighs 800,000 lbs. at take off. It lands at 300,000 lbs. It has consumed 500,000 lbs. fuel with most of that used during take off.[4] Replacing commercial flights less than 300 miles with high speed rail and limiting flights less than 500 miles will save an estimated 3% of total fuel consumed.

Airplanes are major upper atmosphere polluters. It was noted that there was a significant reduction of nitrogen oxides, carbon dioxide and ozone during the few days following September 11, 2001 when general aviation was stopped.

Airplanes will remain a part of our transportation structure for longer distance travel where high speed rail does not compete. Limiting commercial airline flights to longer distances, reducing the number of flights and replacing older aircraft with larger, more efficient planes will reduce fuel consumption and pollution. While the future airline industry will be downsized from its current size, it will become more efficient, reliable and safe.

SUMMARY

The transportation industry can adapt to different energy sources in ways that can help the U.S. attain energy independence. The proposals in this chapter involve major changes in U.S. transportation. These involve smaller automobiles and light trucks with the capability of using a variety of fuels, high speed rail for travel up to 500 miles and reduced air travel.

The solution to energy independence lies in development of alternative fuels. Coal, natural gas and shale oil offer the best opportunities for high energy liquid fuels that can replace liquid petroleum fuels.

---

[4] This is based on a Boeing 747-400 with a maximum takeoff weight of 875,000 lbs. This plane is equipped with four Rolls-Royce RB-211 engines with 59,500 lbs. thrust equivalent to 30 megawatts of power each. These four engines can consume 75,000 lbs. of fuel per hour at full throttle. The plane only operates at full power during take off. The rest of the trip is at reduced throttle. A 12 hour trip consuming 500,000 lbs. fuel is an average of 42,000 lbs. per hour.

Electricity will play an important role in future transportation. Railroads operating on electricity will reduce liquid fuel consumption and pollution. It may be possible to convert long-distance trucks to use electricity through special transportation corridors such as the Tran-Texas Corridor. This is another idea that would require significant investment and time to place in operation.

The American people are logical and will invest in our future transportation requirements as long as they understand the reasons. The proposals presented here will not abridge our freedom to move around the country. Strong leadership at the highest levels will be required to educate and guide us through these changes.

Chapter 6

Maintaining Energy Independence

The ideas put forward in the previous five chapters are a pathway to energy independence for the U.S. There are many interconnecting facets to energy independence. A solution in one area may adversely affect other areas. The purpose of this chapter is to consider the implications of actions suggested in the earlier chapters and how they may interact to change the energy situation in the U.S.

Our goal is to replace all imported petroleum products and natural gas with domestic production, alternative fuels and non-petroleum energy sources by 2020. This will reduce demand on the world market for oil by 14 million barrels per day.

Current world oil production and consumption is 86 million barrels per day and growing at a rate of 2% per year. If we do nothing to change U.S. consumption of petroleum imports, the demand by 2020 will be 109 million barrels per day. If we were to reduce U.S. consumption by 14 million barrels per day, world demand in 2020 from non-U.S. requirements will be 91 million barrels per day.

A net reduction in foreign oil purchases by the U.S. will have an immediate and salutary effect on the world petroleum market. This will cause a temporary collapse of oil prices until world demand absorbs the reduction in foreign oil consumption by the U.S. Development of alternative fuels in the U.S., exporting these fuels - and the technology to produce them - will reduce demand for crude oil thus holding down prices.

POSSIBLE EFFECTS OF APPROACHING AND ACHIEVING ENERGY INDEPENDENCE

If the U.S. is successful in reaching a net reduction of 11 million barrels per day of foreign oil purchases in the short-term and replacing all foreign oil imports with alternative fuels by 2020, the effects could be far reaching. For example:

- Crude oil prices will temporarily collapse – and this could be as low as the cost to produce the oil, perhaps $20 per barrel for a period of

time. As world demand catches up, oil prices will return to present levels or higher.
- With energy independence, the U.S. will not be affected by these developments.
- The U.S. dollar will revalue upwards. The U.S. economy will strengthen and the dollar will return to its status as the international currency.
- The U.S. trade balance will become positive.
- Alternative fuels developed by the U.S. can be sold to other countries improving our balance of payments and taking pressure off oil prices. These actions will strengthen the economies of other oil-importing countries such as the G-7, China and India.
- There will be a substantial reduction in world-wide carbon dioxide production.

The technology developed in reaching U.S. energy independence can be exported to other nations such as China and India to help them achieve energy independence and a cleaner environment. Exportation of technology, engineering and equipment will be positive for our balance of payments.

We can speculate that there will be several interesting political implications:

- There will be a severe curtailment of oil money available to finance terrorism. This could minimize the radical aspects of Islam leading to a much safer world.
- Iran and other oil-producing countries desiring nuclear armament will not have ample income to purchase or develop these weapons programs.
- Oil-producing countries will have restricted funds to purchase arms and delivery systems from North Korea limiting that country's ability to project itself as a nuclear power.
- Venezuela's power and troublemaking capability will be diminished thus limiting the export of socialism in South America.
- Russia will have less money concentrated within a few entities. This will weaken the oligarchy and lead to more democracy and a stronger middle class.
- China's middle class will grow with the availability of lower cost energy. Wages will increase leading to less competitiveness with the U.S. and improvement of our balance of payments position.
- India's economy will move it to the position of a major world player.

We must learn from our past. In the 1980's we returned to high petroleum consumption when oil prices fell to low levels following the embargos in the 1970's. Prices will come down when the U.S. reduces petroleum imports. It is essential that we hold fuel and energy costs at levels that will maintain reduced consumption and promote production of alternative fuels. Once we reach energy independence, it is an absolute requirement that we remain steady on our course.

How to avoid a repeat of the 1980's return to high-energy consumption

European countries are different from the U.S. in many ways and similar in other ways. Europe has a smaller landmass with a higher population and population density than the U.S. Europe has not had the room to build a large highway network like the U.S. Passenger rail travel has remained a viable option and high speed rail has been introduced in many countries in Europe. Governments heavily subsidize passenger rail. In the U.K., passenger service is provided by private companies operating on government owned rail roadbeds. Freight is mostly moved by truck.

Another important difference is that gasoline and Diesel fuels are heavily taxed in Europe. We pay $4 per gallon with about $0.50/gallon state and federal tax; Europeans pay as much as $10 per gallon. Those high taxes and costs for fuel have resulted in different styles of automobiles and trucks that are more fuel-efficient.

Proposals presented in this book would result in the U.S. transportation network evolving to appear more like Europe with high speed passenger trains, fewer intra-city flights and reduced long distance automobile travel. A major difference would be hauling substantial amounts of freight by rail in intermodal service. This will be viable in the U.S. because of the longer travel distances.

Energy consumption is directly related to cost. Therefore, equitable ways must be devised to hold energy costs at a level that will cause the U.S. to continue at a lower energy consumption level.

Taxes on Energy

Taxes on petroleum fuels are currently imposed at the point of purchase by the end user. Let us consider the following proposal. We are currently at about

$140 per barrel and could easily rise to $200 per barrel or higher before these goals begin to take effect. **After crude oil prices start to fall, the cost to refiners for crude oil will be set by Congress at a price holding petroleum fuel costs to the consumer at a fixed level. The difference between the market and set prices paid by refiners will go to the federal government as taxes. Consumer cost for fuel would be commensurate with the fixed price for crude oil.** Similar taxes will be required for alternative fuels based on heat value of the fuel.

If oil were to drop to production cost, as much as $600 billion per year in new tax revenue would go to the federal government. To give some idea of the dollar magnitude, it is approximately 50% of the amount paid by all individuals annually to the federal government in income taxes. This money must be earmarked for a specific purpose. Several hundred billion dollars per year would be too tempting for our politicians to find their favorite project to fund or establish a new entitlement program such as nationalized health care. Possible suggestions are:

Technology. Initially, money should be used to fund technology needed to reach energy independence such as: research and development on fuels from coal, natural gas and shale oil; disposal of nuclear waste; solar power, hydrogen fuel and electricity storage.

Automobile Industry. Imposing 35 mpg CAFE standards on the automobile industry for the 2012 model year will require major design modifications and retooling manufacturing plants. The industry will need assistance through these tumultuous times. Grants for new technology in the area of strong and light weight materials will assist in vehicle weight reductions. The government can offer tax credits to the public for early replacement of low mileage vehicles with more efficient models. Unemployment compensation and retraining can temporarily aid displaced workers. Management, unions and politicians will be called on for flexibility and thinking 'out of the box' to solve these issues.

High Speed Rail and New Freight Lines. Funding will be required for construction of high speed rail. There will be a need for new freight lines including concepts like the Trans Texas Corridor. We fund both interstate highways and airports. There is no reason we cannot subsidize construction of new railroads.

There are existing tracks in the U.S. that, while owned by one railroad, are used by several. This same concept can be used with roads built by the government and shared by any railroad that meets the standards for use.

Highway Construction and Development. Lane separations for trucks and automobiles will improve safety as cars are downsized in weight and size. Separate highways may become necessary for trucks, especially with possible electricity for fuel and multiple trailers. Continued investment in our highway system will be required to maintain and expand as necessary.

National Debt. Pay down the national debt. The current national debt is 9 trillion dollars. At 500 billion dollars per year, the debt would be paid in 18 years.

Social Security. Permanently fund Social Security. Other thoughts on this include privatization and investment of some funds in U.S. companies. Modify Social Security to be more like retirement plans for federal government employees. This will strengthen the U.S. economy and assure people of better retirements.

Reduce Income Taxes. Reduce tax rates and replace the current income tax code with a flat tax. Every American will appreciate being relieved of the task of annually filling out and filing complicated income tax forms.

Reduce Other Taxes. Reduce corporate taxes and eliminate capital gains and inheritance taxes. This will bring U.S. industry to a par with other countries and level the playing field for competition.

Leadership

The leadership of the U.S. has an obligation to establish a plan to be energy independent. While we may have petroleum-based fuels for another fifty years, production cannot keep up with increasing demand and capacity will drop off. To avoid a bitter competition for petroleum, these proposals will guide the U.S. on the path to energy independence and strengthen the democratic gift we received from our forefathers. The American people will respond to this in a positive way if it is adequately explained. We need leadership to present the case and keep us on the path to independence. This leadership must reach across the divide between our political parties. And, it must continue as presidents are elected.

Summary

An essential part of our plan includes maintaining independence once achieved. The cost of energy in the U.S. has been based on world market prices and has been too low in relation to the development of domestic and alternative energy sources. The cost of energy must be maintained at a level that will prevent us from regressing into using large amounts of imported oil and gas as we did in the 1980's.

The proposal to hold the cost of crude oil to a refiner at an artificial level through legislation will fix transportation fuel costs regardless of market price for crude oil. This is different from taxing fuel at the pump which is a fixed amount in addition to market costs. The result will be an enormous cash flow to the federal government. This money must be used wisely and carefully.

Carrying out these proposals will require leadership and communication at the highest levels of government and influence. This will affect our entire population as we adjust to changes. People of all political party affiliations and ideological persuasions must come together to reach the goal of energy independence.

Appendix A

U.S. Energy Supply and Use

The Department of Energy publishes very complete information about sources and uses of energy in the U.S. Published data contain both historical information and future projections.

Table I was derived from Department of Energy sources. All energy values in Table I are in quadrillion (1×10^{15}) Btu's per year (QBtu's). While we normally think of crude oil and other petroleum products in millions of barrels per day, this unit allows an exact comparison of the different energy sources. One million barrels of oil per day are equal to 2.07 QBtu's per year.

The table presents actual consumption in 2005 through 2007 and projected consumption for 2008. Oil prices were projected to be about $80 per barrel in 2008. In the summer of 2008, oil prices exceeded $140 per barrel.

Table Ia was constructed from Table I so that percentages for each source of energy could be calculated for 2007 data. Note that petroleum products are also expressed in units of barrels per day.

In 2007, the U.S. consumed 101.4 QBtu's of energy. In terms of energy consumption, petroleum fluids made up 39.6%, natural gas 23.3%, coal 22.4% and nuclear power 8.2%. The remaining 6.5% was from hydropower, biomass and various renewable energy sources such as wind power. We had a net import of 66% of crude oil consumed and 16.7% of natural gas consumed. In total energy use, we imported 29.4% of our 2007 consumption.

Table I
Total US Energy Supply and Disposition
Quadrillion Btu's per Year

Year	2005	2006	2007	2008
Production				
Crude Oil and Lease Condensate	10.99	10.80	10.98	11.06
Natural Gas Plant Liquids	2.33	2.36	2.38	2.36
Dry Natural Gas	18.60	19.04	19.55	19.73
Coal (1)	23.19	23.79	23.76	23.74
Nuclear Power	8.16	8.21	8.34	8.34
Hydropower	2.70	2.89	2.61	2.70
Biomass (2)	2.79	2.94	3.33	3.83
Other Renewable Energy (3)	0.67	0.88	1.05	1.18
Other (4)	0.36	0.50	0.88	0.69
Total	**69.80**	**71.41**	**72.87**	**73.64**
Imports				
Crude Oil	22.09	22.08	21.79	22.28
Liquid Fuels and Other Petroleum (5)	7.23	7.21	6.87	6.59
Natural Gas	4.45	4.29	4.66	4.66
Other Imports (6)	0.85	0.98	0.93	1.00
Total	**34.62**	**34.57**	**34.25**	**34.53**
Exports				
Petroleum (7)	2.32	2.60	2.74	2.66
Natural Gas	0.74	0.73	0.75	0.71
Coal	1.27	1.26	1.44	1.64
Total	**4.32**	**4.59**	**4.93**	**5.01**
Discrepancy (8)	0.01	1.87	0.79	0.82
Consumption				
Liquid Fuels and Other Petroleum (9)	40.47	40.06	40.19	40.29
Natural Gas	22.65	22.30	23.58	23.79
Coal (10)	22.78	22.50	22.70	22.73
Nuclear Power	8.16	8.21	8.34	8.34
Hydropower	2.70	2.89	2.61	2.70
Biomass (11)	2.45	2.50	2.73	3.09
Other Renewable Energy (3)	0.67	0.88	1.05	1.18
Other (12)	0.21	0.19	0.22	0.22
Total	**100.08**	**99.52**	**101.40**	**102.34**

Table I (Continued)
Quadrillion Btu's per Year

Year	2005	2006	2007	2008
Prices (2006 dollars per unit)				
Petroleum (dollars per barrel)				
Low Sulfur Light Price (13)	58.28	66.02	67.05	83.59
Imported Crude Oil Price (13)	50.40	59.05	62.10	72.77
Natural Gas (dollars per million Btu)				
Price at Henry Hub	8.93	6.73	6.78	7.23
Wellhead Price (14)	7.62	6.24	6.03	6.39
Natural Gas (dollars per thousand cubic feet)				
Wellhead Price (14)	7.85	6.42	6.21	6.58
Coal (dollars per ton)				
Minemouth Price (15)	24.08	24.63	25.45	26.22
Coal (dollars per million Btu)				
Minemouth Price (15)	1.18	1.21	1.25	1.28
Average Delivered Price (16)	1.67	1.78	1.83	1.88
Average Electricity $0.01 per KWH	8.4	8.9	8.9	9.1

1. Includes waste coal.
2. Includes grid-connected electricity from wood and wood waste, biomass such as corn used for liquid fuels production, and non-electric energy from wood.
3. Includes grid-connected electricity from landfill gas; biogenic municipal solid waste; wind; photovoltaic and solar thermal sources, and non-electric energy from renewable sources, such as active and passive solar.
4. Includes non-biogenic municipal solid waste, liquid hydrogen, methanol, and some domestic inputs to refineries.
5. Includes imports of finished petroleum products, unfinished oils, alcohols, ethers, blending components, and renewable fuels such as ethanol.
6. Includes coal, coal coke (net), and electricity (net).
7. Includes crude oil and petroleum products.
8. Balancing item. Includes unaccounted for supply, losses, gains, and net storage withdrawals.
9. Includes petroleum-derived fuels and non-petroleum-derived fuels, such as ethanol, biodiesel, and coal-based synthetic liquids.
10. Excludes coal converted to coal-based synthetic liquids.
11. Includes grid-connected electricity from wood and wood waste, non-electric energy from wood, and biofuels heat and co-products used in the production of liquid fuels, but excludes the energy content of the liquid fuels.
12. Includes non-biogenic municipal solid waste and net electricity imports.
13. Weighted average price delivered to U.S. refiners.
14. Represents Lower 48 onshore and offshore supplies.
15. Includes reported prices for both open market and captive mines.
16. Prices weighted by consumption; weighted average excludes residential and commercial prices, and export free-alongside-ship (f.a.s.) prices.
Btu = British thermal unit.
- - = Not applicable.
Note: Totals may not equal sum of components due to independent rounding. Data for 2005 and 2006 are model results and may differ slightly from official EIA data reports.
Report #: DOE/EIA-0383 (2008)

Table Ia
U.S. Energy Supply and Disposition (2007)

Year	Quadrillion Btu's	Million Barrels per day	%
Production			
Crude Oil and Lease Condensate	10.98	5.30	10.8%
Natural Gas Plant Liquids	2.38	1.15	2.3%
Dry Natural Gas	19.55		19.3%
Coal	23.76		23.4%
Nuclear Power	8.34		8.2%
Hydropower	2.61		2.6%
Biomass	3.33		3.3%
Other Renewable Energy	1.05		1.0%
Other	0.88		0.9%
Total	**72.87**	**6.45**	
Imports			
Crude Oil	21.79	10.53	21.5%
Liquid Fuels and Other Petroleum	6.87	3.32	6.8%
Natural Gas	4.66		4.6%
Other Imports	0.93		0.9%
Total	**34.25**	**13.85**	
Exports			
Petroleum	2.74	1.32	2.7%
Natural Gas	0.75		0.7%
Coal	1.44		1.4%
Total	**4.93**	**1.32**	
Discrepancy from EIA Data	**0.93**	**0.45**	
Consumption			
Liquid Fuels and Other Petroleum	40.19	19.42	39.6%
Natural Gas	23.58		23.3%
Coal	22.70		22.4%
Nuclear Power	8.34		8.2%
Hydropower	2.61		2.6%
Biomass	2.73		2.7%
Other Renewable Energy	1.05		1.0%
Other	0.22		0.2%
Total	**101.40**	**19.42**	

Report #: DOE/EIA-0383 (2008)

Appendix B

Sources of Petroleum

PETROLEUM RESERVES

Table II presents proven World Petroleum Reserves by country. This table shows every country with any proven reserve, no matter how small. It can be seen from this table that the Middle East dominates the list with 739 billion barrels of reserves. North America is at a distant second place with 213 billion barrels followed by Africa, South America, Eurasia, Asia-Oceania and Europe in that order.

Table IIa presents proven reserves by country down to 0.1 billion barrels beginning with the largest. As expected, Saudi Arabia tops the list with 20% of known reserves. It is followed by Canada with 13.6% and Iran with 10.3%. Venezuela is in 7th place, Russia in 8th and the United States at a surprising 12th place ahead of China at 13th place. The two countries with enormous future potential for consumption of oil are China and India at 21st indicating that they will be large net importers of oil.

The top 20 (ending with Azerbaijan) have 95% of reserves. The remaining countries have a summed total of 5% of reserves. Some of those countries have sufficient oil to meet their domestic needs; others do not.

OPEC Countries vs. Non-OPEC Countries

Table IIb presents the data comparing reserves in OPEC countries with Non-OPEC countries. OPEC countries have 69.7% of world reserves, led by Saudi Arabia with 28.7% of total OPEC reserves. Qatar and Algeria, in 9th and 10th places, have reserves in the range of China and Mexico in the Non-OPEC list. Indonesia is a minor player and its reserves are between the 12th and 13th on the Non-OPEC list. Reserves in the Gulf Region are 79% of the OPEC total and 54.4% of total world reserves. It is not a reassuring prospect to depend on that level of reserves in an unreliable and unstable part of the world.

The Non-OPEC list is dominated by Canada and Russia with 60.3% of Non-OPEC reserves. The U.S., in fourth place after Kazakhstan, has 5.5% compared with China at 4.0%, Mexico at 3.1% and Brazil at 3.0%.

U.S. Petroleum Reserves

Table III presents U.S. reserves by state for the years 2001 through 2006. U.S. proven reserves have drifted down from 22,446 to 20,972 billion barrels during this period. This table does not differentiate between offshore and onshore production. It can be seen that production is dominated by Alaska, California and Texas.

Table IIIa presents a more complete breakout with percentages. Federal Offshore is for leases owned by the federal government. The government controls 19.5% of U.S. reserves. California, Louisiana and Texas have some offshore leases amounting to about 1.2% of total reserves.

Table IIIb lists reserves by state and federal area. Texas, Alaska, Federal Gulf of Mexico (off Louisiana) and California dominate the list. It is obvious from this list that additional production can come from Alaska and offshore. Texas production is older, but can still be viable through tertiary recovery and well stimulation. This does not include new finds in South Dakota and other areas.

These data say nothing about unproven reserves offshore around Florida and the east coast, and off Washington and Oregon. There is extreme pressure from environmentalist groups not to drill off the coasts of the areas named above.

WORLD PETROLEUM PRODUCTION

Table IV presents world production of crude oil, natural gas production liquids and petroleum liquids by country and region. Production does not follow the pattern of reserves indicating that countries with large reserves are not as well developed as countries with older production. As expected, the Middle East leads with 25.6 million barrels per day followed by North America at 15.2 million barrels per day.

World production in 2005 is presented by country in Table IVa. Of the thirty-three countries that make up 95.2% of world production, ten of the thirteen OPEC countries dominate the list. The U.S. is third after Russia and ahead of Iran. Canada is 7th even though it has the 2nd largest reserves in the world.

OPEC and Non-OPEC countries are compared in Table IVb. Non-OPEC countries make up 57.5% of production compared with 42.5% for OPEC. This is not a good indicator for the future since productions and reserves are reversed in the two sets of countries. Non-OPEC countries have already peaked in production as is the case of the U.S. or will peak in the next decade or two.

World production by region is presented in Table IVc. This shows consistent growth in the Middle East, Asia Oceania, Africa, Central & South America and Europe with North America fairly constant. This, again, shows the peaking effect in mature producing areas.

U.S. IMPORTS BY COUNTRY OF ORIGIN

Table V gives imports by country of origin separating OPEC and Non-OPEC countries. **In 2007, 44.5% of the oil the U.S. imported came from OPEC countries.** Principle suppliers were Nigeria, Saudi Arabia and Venezuela with roughly 1.3 million barrels per day each. Table Va presents U.S. imports by country. The top five countries were Canada, Mexico, Saudi Arabia, Venezuela and Nigeria. There is some comfort that 90% of our imported oil comes from an aggregate total of 20 countries.

Table II
World Proved Reserves of Oil (2007) - Region

Country and Region	Oil (Billion Barrels)
Canada	179.210
Mexico	12.352
United States	21.757
North America	**213.319**
Argentina	2.468
Barbados	0.003
Belize	0.007
Bolivia	0.440
Brazil	11.773
Chile	0.150
Colombia	1.453
Cuba	0.124
Ecuador	4.517
Guatemala	0.083
Peru	0.930
Suriname	0.111
Trinidad and Tobago	0.728
Venezuela	80.012
Central & South America	**102.798**
Albania	0.198
Austria	0.050
Bulgaria	0.015
Croatia	0.074
Czech Republic	0.015
Denmark	1.277
France	0.122
Germany	0.367
Greece	0.005
Hungary	0.020
Italy	0.600
Netherlands	0.100
Norway	7.849
Poland	0.096
Romania	0.600
Serbia and Montenegro	0.078
Slovakia	0.009
Spain	0.150
Turkey	0.300
United Kingdom	3.875
Europe	**15.800**

Table II (Continued)

Country/Region	Oil (Billion Barrels)
Azerbaijan	7.000
Belarus	0.198
Georgia	0.035
Kazakhstan	30.000
Kyrgyzstan	0.040
Lithuania	0.012
Russia	60.000
Tajikistan	0.012
Turkmenistan	0.600
Ukraine	0.395
Uzbekistan	0.594
Eurasia	**98.886**
Bahrain	0.125
Iran	136.270
Iraq	115.000
Israel	0.002
Jordan	0.001
Kuwait	101.500
Oman	5.500
Qatar	15.207
Saudi Arabia	262.300
Syria	2.500
United Arab Emirates	97.800
Yemen	3.000
Middle East	**739.205**
Algeria	12.270
Angola	8.000
Benin	0.008
Cameroon	0.400
Chad	1.500
Congo (Brazzaville)	1.600
Congo (Kinshasa)	0.180
Cote d'Ivoire (IvoryCoast)	0.100
Egypt	3.700
Equatorial Guinea	1.100
Gabon	2.000
Ghana	0.015
Libya	41.464
Mauritania	0.100
Morocco	0.001
Nigeria	36.220
South Africa	0.015
Sudan	5.000
Tunisia	0.400
Africa	**114.073**

Table II (Continued)

Country/Region	Oil (Billion Barrels)
Australia	1.592
Bangladesh	0.028
Brunei	1.100
Burma	0.050
China	16.000
India	5.625
Indonesia	4.300
Japan	0.059
Malaysia	3.000
New Zealand	0.053
Pakistan	0.289
Papua New Guinea	0.240
Philippines	0.139
Taiwan	0.002
Thailand	0.290
Vietnam	0.600
Asia & Oceania	**33.366**
World Total	**1,317.447**

2005 Annual Report, DOE/EIA-0216(2005) (November 2006).

Table IIa
World Proved Reserves of Oil (2007) - Country

	Country	Oil (Billion Barrels)	Percent	Cumulative
1	Saudi Arabia	262.300	19.9%	19.9%
2	Canada	179.210	13.6%	33.5%
3	Iran	136.270	10.3%	43.9%
4	Iraq	115.000	8.7%	52.6%
5	Kuwait	101.500	7.7%	60.3%
6	United Arab Emirates	97.800	7.4%	67.7%
7	Venezuela	80.012	6.1%	73.8%
8	Russia	60.000	4.6%	78.3%
9	Libya	41.464	3.1%	81.5%
10	Nigeria	36.220	2.7%	84.2%
11	Kazakhstan	30.000	2.3%	86.5%
12	United States	21.757	1.7%	88.2%
13	China	16.000	1.2%	89.4%
14	Qatar	15.207	1.2%	90.5%
15	Mexico	12.352	0.9%	91.5%
16	Algeria	12.270	0.9%	92.4%
17	Brazil	11.773	0.9%	93.3%
18	Angola	8.000	0.6%	93.9%
19	Norway	7.849	0.6%	94.5%
20	Azerbaijan	7.000	0.5%	95.0%
21	India	5.625	0.4%	95.5%
22	Oman	5.500	0.4%	95.9%
23	Sudan	5.000	0.4%	96.3%
24	Ecuador	4.517	0.3%	96.6%
25	Indonesia	4.300	0.3%	96.9%
26	United Kingdom	3.875	0.3%	97.2%
27	Egypt	3.700	0.3%	97.5%
28	Yemen	3.000	0.2%	97.7%
29	Malaysia	3.000	0.2%	98.0%
30	Syria	2.500	0.2%	98.1%
31	Argentina	2.468	0.2%	98.3%
32	Gabon	2.000	0.2%	98.5%
33	Congo (Brazzaville)	1.600	0.1%	98.6%
34	Australia	1.592	0.1%	98.7%
35	Chad	1.500	0.1%	98.8%
36	Colombia	1.453	0.1%	98.9%
37	Denmark	1.277	0.1%	99.0%
	World Total	**1,317.447**		

2005 Annual Report, DOE/EIA-0216(2005) (November 2006).

Table IIb
World Proved Reserves of Oil (2007)
OPEC and Non-OPEC Countries

	Country/Region	Oil (Billion Barrels)	Percent	Cumulative
	OPEC Countries			
1	Saudi Arabia	262.300	28.7%	28.7%
2	Iran	136.270	14.9%	43.6%
3	Iraq	115.000	12.6%	56.1%
4	Kuwait	101.500	11.1%	67.2%
5	United Arab Emirates	97.800	10.7%	77.9%
6	Venezuela	80.012	8.7%	86.7%
7	Libya	41.464	4.5%	91.2%
8	Nigeria	36.220	4.0%	95.2%
9	Qatar	15.207	1.7%	96.8%
10	Algeria	12.270	1.3%	98.2%
11	Angola	8.000	0.9%	99.0%
12	Ecuador	4.517	0.5%	99.5%
13	Indonesia	4.300	0.5%	100.0%
	OPEC Total	**914.860**	**69.7%**	
	Non-OPEC Countries			
1	Canada	179.210	45.1%	45.1%
2	Russia	60.000	15.1%	60.3%
3	Kazakhstan	30.000	7.6%	67.8%
4	United States	21.757	5.5%	73.3%
5	China	16.000	4.0%	77.3%
6	Mexico	12.352	3.1%	80.4%
7	Brazil	11.773	3.0%	83.4%
8	Norway	7.849	2.0%	85.4%
9	Azerbaijan	7.000	1.8%	87.1%
10	India	5.625	1.4%	88.6%
11	Oman	5.500	1.4%	89.9%
12	Sudan	5.000	1.3%	91.2%
13	United Kingdom	3.875	1.0%	92.2%
14	Egypt	3.700	0.9%	93.1%
15	Yemen	3.000	0.8%	93.9%
16	Malaysia	3.000	0.8%	94.6%
17	Syria	2.500	0.6%	95.2%
18	Argentina	2.468	0.6%	95.9%
19	Gabon	2.000	0.5%	96.4%
20	Congo (Brazzaville)	1.600	0.4%	96.8%
21	Australia	1.592	0.4%	97.2%
	Non-OPEC Total	**397.014**	**30.3%**	

2005 Annual Report, DOE/EIA-0216(2005) (November 2006).

Table III
U.S. Oil Reserves By State
(Billion Barrels)

	2001	2002	2003	2004	2005	2006
U.S. Total	22,446	22,677	21,891	21,371	21,757	20,972
Alaska	4,851	4,678	4,446	4,327	4,171	3,879
Alabama	42	51	52	53	55	45
Arkansas	43	49	50	51	40	37
California	3,627	3,633	3,452	3,376	3,435	3,389
Colorado	196	214	217	225	250	274
Florida	75	73	68	65	59	38
Illinois	92	107	125	92	95	89
Indiana	12	15	19	11	16	12
Kansas	216	237	243	245	281	263
Kentucky	17	27	25	27	23	25
Louisiana	564	501	452	427	432	428
Michigan	46	61	75	53	62	63
Mississippi	167	179	169	178	189	186
Montana	260	288	315	364	427	419
Nebraska	15	18	16	15	16	14
New Mexico	715	710	677	669	690	705
North Dakota	328	342	353	389	418	412
Ohio	46	67	66	49	46	49
Oklahoma	556	598	588	570	630	569
Pennsylvania	10	12	13	12	14	20
Texas	4,944	5,015	4,583	4,613	4,919	4,871
Utah	271	241	221	215	256	334
West Virginia	8	13	13	11	21	23
Wyoming	489	524	517	628	704	706
Miscellaneous	21	15	16	15	25	26

Energy Information Agency, Department of Energy, 2006 Report.

U.S. Crude Oil Reserves

Table IIIa
U.S. Oil Reserves by State and Region (2006)

	State (Billion Barrels)	Offshore	Percent	
U.S. Total	**20,972**			
Federal Offshore	4,096		19.5%	
Pacific (California)		441		2.1%
Gulf of Mexico (Louisiana)		3,500		16.7%
Gulf of Mexico (Texas)		155		0.7%
Alaska	3,879		18.5%	
Alabama	45		0.2%	
Arkansas	37		0.2%	
California	3,389		16.2%	
CA State Offshore		202		1.0%
Colorado	274		1.3%	
Florida	38		0.2%	
Illinois	89		0.4%	
Indiana	12		0.1%	
Kansas	263		1.3%	
Kentucky	25		0.1%	
Louisiana	428		2.0%	
LA State Offshore		48		0.2%
Michigan	63		0.3%	
Mississippi	186		0.9%	
Montana	419		2.0%	
Nebraska	14		0.1%	
New Mexico	705		3.4%	
North Dakota	412		2.0%	
Ohio	49		0.2%	
Oklahoma	569		2.7%	
Pennsylvania	20		0.1%	
Texas	4,871		23.2%	
TX State Offshore		3		0.0%
Utah	334		1.6%	
West Virginia	23		0.1%	
Wyoming	706		3.4%	
Miscellaneous	26		0.1%	

Energy Information Agency, Department of Energy, 2006 Report.
U.S. Crude Oil Reserves

Table IIIb
U.S. Oil Reserves by Volume

		Amount (Billion Barrels)	Percentage	Cumulative
1	Texas	4,871	23.2%	23.2%
2	Alaska	3,879	18.5%	41.7%
3	Federal Gulf of Mexico (LA)	3,500	16.7%	58.4%
4	California	3,389	16.2%	74.6%
5	Wyoming	706	3.4%	77.9%
6	New Mexico	705	3.4%	81.3%
7	Oklahoma	569	2.7%	84.0%
8	Federal Offshore Pacific (CA)	441	2.1%	86.1%
9	Louisiana	428	2.0%	88.2%
10	Montana	419	2.0%	90.2%
11	North Dakota	412	2.0%	92.1%
12	Utah	334	1.6%	93.7%
13	Colorado	274	1.3%	95.0%
14	Kansas	263	1.3%	96.3%
15	Mississippi	186	0.9%	97.2%
16	Federal Gulf of Mexico (TX)	155	0.7%	97.9%
17	Illinois	89	0.4%	98.3%
18	Michigan	63	0.3%	98.6%
19	Ohio	49	0.2%	98.9%
20	Alabama	45	0.2%	99.1%
21	Florida	38	0.2%	99.3%
22	Arkansas	37	0.2%	99.4%
23	Miscellaneous	26	0.1%	99.6%
24	Kentucky	25	0.1%	99.7%
25	West Virginia	23	0.1%	99.8%
26	Pennsylvania	20	0.1%	99.9%
27	Nebraska	14	0.1%	99.9%
28	Indiana	12	0.1%	100.0%
	U.S. Total	**20,972**		

Energy Information Agency, Department of Energy, 2006 Report.
U.S. Crude Oil Reserves

Table IV
World Production of Crude Oil and Other Liquids
(Thousand Barrels per Day)

Country	1980	1985	1990	1995	2000	2005
Canada	1,816	1,848	2,040	2,453	2,749	3,092
Mexico	2,129	3,027	2,992	3,075	3,460	3,784
United States	10,809	11,192	9,678	9,400	9,058	8,322
North America	**14,754**	**16,068**	**14,709**	**14,928**	**15,267**	**15,198**
Argentina	508	485	521	774	832	802
Aruba	- -	- -	(0)	-	2	2
Barbados	-	2	1	1	2	1
Bolivia	32	26	26	35	40	63
Brazil	245	734	821	925	1,543	2,038
Chile	46	48	35	26	16	15
Colombia	134	182	454	597	704	539
Cuba	6	19	12	26	43	81
Dominican Republic	1	1	(0)	(1)	(0)	(0)
Ecuador	207	284	286	396	396	533
Guatemala	5	3	4	9	21	17
Netherlands Antilles	4	4	(1)	(1)	(1)	(0)
Panama	1	-	(0)	0	(1)	-
Peru	200	193	128	130	100	111
Puerto Rico	-	(1)	2	2	0	1
Suriname	-	1	4	7	10	9
Trinidad and Tobago	214	178	149	138	145	181
Uruguay	-	-	0	(0)	0	1
Venezuela	2,246	1,757	2,262	2,982	3,461	2,863
Virgin Islands, U.S.	-	0	(1)	10	15	18
Central & So. America	**3,848**	**3,916**	**4,703**	**6,056**	**7,326**	**7,273**
Albania	44	55	30	10	6	7
Austria	30	25	27	28	24	23
Belgium	8	11	11	12	10	9
Bulgaria	3	6	3	1	2	4
Croatia	- -	- -	- -	42	33	27
Czech Republic	- -	- -	- -	4	8	18
Denmark	5	58	121	187	365	379
Finland	(0)	4	6	9	8	9
Former Czechoslovakia	2	(4)	1	- -	- -	- -
Former Serbia	- -	- -	- -	23	17	14
Former Yugoslavia	88	90	72	- -	- -	- -
France	83	106	112	110	85	73
Germany	- -	- -	- -	138	147	142
Germany, East	(6)	1	4	- -	- -	- -
Germany, West	124	148	151	- -	- -	- -
Greece	1	30	19	12	8	6
Hungary	58	63	58	60	49	42

Table IV (Continued)

Country	1980	1985	1990	1995	2000	2005
Italy	68	84	109	126	133	165
Netherlands	31	101	108	118	88	84
Norway	529	827	1,725	2,910	3,355	2,978
Poland	8	6	5	8	21	33
Portugal	(3)	(1)	(0)	3	2	4
Romania	252	235	167	149	137	123
Slovakia	- -	- -	- -	2	3	13
Spain	13	40	37	32	22	29
Sweden	(6)	0	2	2	2	2
Switzerland	1	2	1	2	2	3
Turkey	41	40	70	66	51	45
United Kingdom	1,674	2,711	1,982	2,819	2,567	1,861
Europe	**3,048**	**4,638**	**4,818**	**6,872**	**7,145**	**6,094**
Azerbaijan	- -	- -	- -	181	289	441
Belarus	- -	- -	- -	34	35	34
Estonia	- -	- -	- -	-	5	7
Former U.S.S.R.	11,991	11,935	11,301	- -	- -	- -
Georgia	- -	- -	- -	1	2	2
Kazakhstan	- -	- -	- -	415	726	1,338
Kyrgyzstan	- -	- -	- -	2	2	2
Lithuania	- -	- -	- -	6	10	13
Russia	- -	- -	- -	6,172	6,724	9,513
Tajikistan	- -	- -	- -	1	0	0
Turkmenistan	- -	- -	- -	82	157	197
Ukraine	- -	- -	- -	82	91	100
Uzbekistan	- -	- -	- -	160	152	125
Eurasia	**11,991**	**11,935**	**11,301**	**7,136**	**8,191**	**11,772**
Bahrain	57	49	48	53	50	48
Iran	1,683	2,272	3,113	3,709	3,765	4,238
Iraq	2,526	1,447	2,064	580	2,582	1,887
Israel	35	1	1	3	4	6
Jordan	-	-	1	0	(0)	(0)
Kuwait	1,760	1,086	1,234	2,159	2,201	2,669
Oman	284	502	693	859	972	780
Qatar	483	332	448	499	875	1,111
Saudi Arabia	10,285	3,778	7,019	9,235	9,476	11,096
Syria	164	178	385	584	547	479
United Arab Emirates	1,747	1,356	2,252	2,396	2,572	2,845
Yemen	-	-	191	345	437	402
Middle East	**19,024**	**11,001**	**17,449**	**20,421**	**23,480**	**25,559**

Table IV (Continued)

Country	1980	1985	1990	1995	2000	2005
Algeria	1,143	1,158	1,305	1,347	1,483	2,090
Angola	150	231	474	645	746	1,260
Benin	-	8	4	3	1	-
Cameroon	58	185	161	111	85	83
Chad	-	-	-	-	-	177
Congo (Brazzaville)	65	120	165	188	292	236
Congo (Kinshasa)	20	33	29	30	26	20
Cote d'Ivoire (IvoryCoast)	2	29	2	8	12	58
Egypt	613	915	901	929	793	688
Equatorial Guinea	-	-	-	5	168	396
Ghana	2	1	(0)	4	7	8
Kenya	1	1	(0)	0	(0)	(0)
Libya	1,827	1,085	1,407	1,428	1,469	1,721
Morocco	2	2	(1)	(1)	4	4
Nigeria	2,060	1,500	1,817	1,998	2,169	2,630
South Africa	-	60	77	207	202	217
Sudan	-	-	0	0	187	352
Tunisia	110	114	98	90	80	77
Africa	**6,229**	**5,615**	**6,708**	**7,357**	**8,039**	**10,283**
Australia	460	665	666	647	828	572
Bangladesh	-	1	1	1	3	7
Brunei	270	168	160	176	215	214
Burma	30	30	14	10	13	21
China	2,114	2,505	2,768	3,060	3,378	3,781
East Timor	- -	- -	- -	- -	- -	94
Korea, South	-	(9)	(10)	(22)	14	17
Malaysia	284	451	630	718	771	752
New Zealand	9	24	59	48	48	28
Pakistan	11	36	62	62	57	68
Papua New Guinea	-	-	-	100	70	40
Philippines	16	10	4	3	(0)	24
Singapore	4	4	(6)	(1)	13	10
Sri Lanka	-	-	(0)	(0)	(0)	(1)
Taiwan	9	6	(5)	(7)	(6)	11
Thailand	1	53	58	92	182	311
Vietnam	-	-	50	173	316	375
Asia & Oceania	**5,093**	**6,000**	**6,736**	**7,501**	**8,313**	**8,437**
World Total	**63,987**	**59,172**	**66,426**	**70,272**	**77,762**	**84,615**

Energy Information Administration, International Energy Annual 2005
Table Posted: August 6, 2007.

Table IVa
World Production of Crude Oil by Volume
(Thousand Barrels per Day)

	Country	2005	Percent	Cumulative
1	Saudi Arabia	11,096	13.5%	13.5%
2	Russia	9,513	11.6%	25.1%
3	United States	8,322	10.1%	35.2%
4	Iran	4,238	5.2%	40.3%
5	Mexico	3,784	4.6%	44.9%
6	China	3,781	4.6%	49.5%
7	Canada	3,092	3.8%	53.3%
8	Norway	2,978	3.6%	56.9%
9	Venezuela	2,863	3.5%	60.4%
10	United Arab Emirates	2,845	3.5%	63.9%
11	Kuwait	2,669	3.2%	67.1%
12	Nigeria	2,630	3.2%	70.3%
13	Algeria	2,090	2.5%	72.8%
14	Brazil	2,038	2.5%	75.3%
15	Iraq	1,887	2.3%	77.6%
16	United Kingdom	1,861	2.3%	79.9%
17	Libya	1,721	2.1%	82.0%
18	Kazakhstan	1,338	1.6%	83.6%
19	Angola	1,260	1.5%	85.1%
20	Qatar	1,111	1.4%	86.5%
21	Argentina	802	1.0%	87.4%
22	Oman	780	0.9%	88.4%
23	Malaysia	752	0.9%	89.3%
24	Egypt	688	0.8%	90.1%
25	Australia	572	0.7%	90.8%
26	Colombia	539	0.7%	91.5%
27	Ecuador	533	0.6%	92.1%
28	Syria	479	0.6%	92.7%
29	Azerbaijan	441	0.5%	93.3%
30	Yemen	402	0.5%	93.8%
31	Equatorial Guinea	396	0.5%	94.2%
32	Denmark	379	0.5%	94.7%
33	Vietnam	375	0.5%	95.2%
	Total	82,240		

Energy Information Administration, International Energy Annual 2005
Table Posted: August 6, 2007.

Table IVb
World Production of Crude Oil - OPEC vs. Non-OPEC Countries
(Thousand Barrels per Day)

	Country	2005	Percent	Cumulative
	OPEC Countries			
1	Saudi Arabia	11,096	31.8%	31.8%
2	Iran	4,238	12.1%	43.9%
3	Venezuela	2,863	8.2%	52.1%
4	United Arab Emirates	2,845	8.1%	60.2%
5	Kuwait	2,669	7.6%	67.9%
6	Nigeria	2,630	7.5%	75.4%
7	Algeria	2,090	6.0%	81.4%
8	Iraq	1,887	5.4%	86.8%
9	Libya	1,721	4.9%	91.7%
10	Angola	1,260	3.6%	95.3%
11	Qatar	1,111	3.2%	98.5%
12	Ecuador	533	1.5%	100.0%
	Total OPEC Countries	34,942	42.5%	
	Non-OPEC Countries			
1	Russia	9,513	20.1%	20.1%
2	United States	8,322	17.6%	37.7%
3	Mexico	3,784	8.0%	45.7%
4	China	3,781	8.0%	53.7%
5	Canada	3,092	6.5%	60.2%
6	Norway	2,978	6.3%	66.5%
7	Brazil	2,038	4.3%	70.8%
8	United Kingdom	1,861	3.9%	74.8%
9	Kazakhstan	1,338	2.8%	77.6%
10	Argentina	802	1.7%	97.0%
11	Oman	780	1.6%	98.6%
12	Malaysia	752	1.6%	100.2%
13	Egypt	688	1.5%	101.7%
14	Australia	572	1.2%	102.9%
15	Colombia	539	1.1%	104.0%
16	Syria	479	1.0%	101.0%
	Total Non-OPEC Countries	47,297	57.5%	
	World Total	82,240		

Energy Information Administration, International Energy Annual 2005
Table Posted: August 6, 2007.

Table IVc
World Production by Region
(Thousand Barrels per Day)

Region	1980	1985	1990	1995	2000	2005
Middle East	19,024	11,001	17,449	20,421	23,480	25,559
North America	14,754	16,068	14,709	14,928	15,267	15,198
Asia & Oceania	5,093	6,000	6,736	7,501	8,313	8,437
Eurasia	11,991	11,935	11,301	7,136	8,191	11,772
Africa	6,229	5,615	6,708	7,357	8,039	10,283
Cent. & So. America	3,848	3,916	4,703	6,056	7,326	7,273
Europe	3,048	4,638	4,818	6,872	7,145	6,094
World Total	63,987	59,172	66,426	70,272	77,762	84,615

Energy Information Administration, International Energy Annual 2005
Table Posted: August 6, 2007.

Table V
U.S. Imports by Country of Origin
OPEC vs. Non-OPEC
(Thousand Barrels per Day)

Year	2002	2005	2007	Percent
All Countries	11,530	13,714	13,439	
Persian Gulf	2,269	2,334	2,170	16.1%
OPEC	4,605	5,587	5,983	44.5%
Algeria	264	478	670	5.0%
Angola	332	473	507	3.8%
Ecuador	110	283	203	1.5%
Indonesia	53	24	28	0.2%
Iran				0.0%
Iraq	459	531	485	3.6%
Kuwait	228	243	183	1.4%
Libya		56	116	0.9%
Nigeria	621	1,166	1,132	8.4%
Qatar	15	4	2	0.0%
Saudi Arabia	1,552	1,537	1,489	11.1%
United Arab Emirates	15	18	10	0.1%
Venezuela	1,398	1,529	1,362	10.1%
Non-OPEC	6,925	8,127	7,456	55.5%
Albania		1		0.0%
Argentina	115	102	64	0.5%
Aruba		125	110	0.8%
Australia	57	14	4	0.0%
Austria				0.0%
Azerbaijan	0	2	62	0.5%
Bahamas	34	32	4	0.0%
Bahrain			1	0.0%
Barbados				0.0%
Belarus		3	19	0.1%
Belgium	71	77	85	0.6%
Belize			1	0.0%
Benin				0.0%
Bolivia		1	3	0.0%
Brazil	116	156	202	1.5%
Brunei	10	14	11	0.1%
Bulgaria	1	1	4	0.0%
Burma				0.0%
Cameroon	13	8	30	0.2%
Canada	1,971	2,181	2,426	18.1%
Chad		97	78	0.6%
Chile	4	17	6	0.0%
China	26	33	13	0.1%

Table V (Continued)

Year	2002	2005	2007	Percent
China, Taiwan	7	21	20	0.1%
Colombia	260	196	154	1.1%
Congo (Brazzaville)	28	32	64	0.5%
Congo (Kinshasa)	3	2	1	0.0%
Costa Rica	1	2	3	0.0%
Denmark	4	7	6	0.0%
Egypt	11	15	9	0.1%
El Salvador		2	5	0.0%
Equatorial Guinea	45	70	58	0.4%
Estonia	12	33	16	0.1%
Finland	18	15	25	0.2%
France	24	62	71	0.5%
Gabon	143	128	65	0.5%
Georgia, Republic of	0	2	2	0.0%
Germany	40	74	71	0.5%
Ghana	2	2	1	0.0%
Greece	2	2	4	0.0%
Guatemala	23	11	11	0.1%
Hungary	0	0	0	0.0%
India	21	28	29	0.2%
Ireland	3	5	2	0.0%
Israel	5	5	3	0.0%
Italy	34	43	55	0.4%
Ivory Coast	6	24	1	0.0%
Jamaica	0	2	5	0.0%
Japan	7	11	35	0.3%
Kazakhstan		21	19	0.1%
Korea, South	45	63	123	0.9%
Latvia	7	24	11	0.1%
Lithuania	9	22	10	0.1%
Malaysia	16	22	14	0.1%
Malta	0	1		0.0%
Mauritania			3	0.0%
Mexico	1,547	1,662	1,533	11.4%
Midway Islands		1	0	0.0%
Morocco	1	2	2	0.0%
Nambia				0.0%
Netherlands	66	151	127	0.9%
Netherlands Antilles	81	29	9	0.1%
New Zealand				0.0%
Norway	393	233	141	1.0%
Oman	17	24	32	0.2%
Pakistan				0.0%

Table V (Continued)

Year	2002	2005	2007	Percent
Panama	1		1	0.0%
Papua New Guinea	4			0.0%
Peru	23	35	34	0.3%
Philippines		0	1	0.0%
Poland		0	1	0.0%
Portugal	10	9	25	0.2%
Puerto Rico	0	0		0.0%
Romania	15	4	1	0.0%
Russia	210	410	413	3.1%
Senegal				0.0%
Singapore	19	14	12	0.1%
Slovakia				0.0%
South Africa	1	1	7	0.1%
Spain	17	28	53	0.4%
Spatly Islands			0	0.0%
Swaziland				0.0%
Sweden	16	26	24	0.2%
Switzerland	0	0	0	0.0%
Syria	11	12	4	0.0%
Thailand	2	3	16	0.1%
Togo				0.0%
Tonga				0.0%
Trinidad and Tobago	80	112	99	0.7%
Tunisia	1	4	14	0.1%
Turkey	13	21	13	0.1%
Turkmenistan	1	4	5	0.0%
Ukraine		2	1	0.0%
United Kingdom	478	396	278	2.1%
Uruguay		3	1	0.0%
Vietnam	21	31	31	0.2%
Virgin Islands (U.S.)	236	328	346	2.6%
Yemen	27	13	13	0.1%

Energy Information Agency, Dept. of Energy, "U.S. Government, Imports by Area of Entry." http://tonto.eia.doe.gov/dnav/pet/pet_move_imp_dc_NUS-ZOO_mbblpd_a.htm

Table Va
U.S. Imports by Country
(Thousand Barrels per Day)

Year	2007	%	Cumulative
All Countries	13,439		
OPEC	5,983	44.5%	
Non-OPEC	7,456	55.5%	
Canada	2,426	18.1%	18.1%
Mexico	1,533	11.4%	29.5%
Saudi Arabia - OPEC	1,489	11.1%	40.5%
Venezuela - OPEC	1,362	10.1%	50.7%
Nigeria - OPEC	1,132	8.4%	59.1%
Algeria - OPEC	670	5.0%	64.1%
Angola - OPEC	507	3.8%	67.9%
Iraq - OPEC	485	3.6%	71.5%
Russia	413	3.1%	74.5%
Virgin Islands (U.S.)	346	2.6%	77.1%
United Kingdom	278	2.1%	79.2%
Ecuador - OPEC	203	1.5%	80.7%
Brazil	202	1.5%	82.2%
Kuwait - OPEC	183	1.4%	83.6%
Colombia	154	1.1%	84.7%
Norway	141	1.0%	85.8%
Netherlands	127	0.9%	86.7%
Korea, South	123	0.9%	87.6%
Libya - OPEC	116	0.9%	88.5%
Aruba	110	0.8%	89.3%
Trinidad and Tobago	99	0.7%	90.0%
Belgium	85	0.6%	90.7%
Chad	78	0.6%	91.2%
France	71	0.5%	91.8%
Germany	71	0.5%	92.3%
Gabon	65	0.5%	92.8%
Argentina	64	0.5%	93.3%
Congo (Brazzaville)	64	0.5%	93.7%
Azerbaijan	62	0.5%	94.2%
Equatorial Guinea	58	0.4%	94.6%
Italy	55	0.4%	95.0%
Spain	53	0.4%	95.4%
Japan	35	0.3%	95.7%
Peru	34	0.3%	95.9%

Energy Information Agency, Dept. of Energy, "U.S. Government, Imports by Area of Entry."
http://tonto.eia.doe.gov/dnav/pet/pet_move_imp_dc_NUS-ZOO_mbblpd_a.htm

Appendix C

U.S. Refineries and Capacities

Table I in Appendix A shows that 40.4% of U.S. energy consumption in 2007 was in the form of refined petroleum products. Appendix C will examine U.S. refineries, their locations and output from these refineries.

It is often pointed out that there has not been a new refinery built in the United States in over 25 years. While this is true, here have been major expansions at existing locations. There are 143 operating refineries in the U.S. with a total capacity of 17,443,492 barrels per day. This is a significant increase in refining capacity over the past quarter century. **More troublesome is the fact that the U.S. consumed 19.4 million barrels per day of petroleum products in 2007. This is a shortfall of 2 million barrels per day refining capacity.**

All U.S. operating refineries are listed in Table VI. The top 62 have a capacity of over 100,000 barrels per day and 111 have a capacity of 30,000 barrels per day or higher.

U.S. refining capabilities are spread out over a large number of installations. The two largest, ExxonMobil at Baytown, TX and Baton Rouge, LA have capacities of 562,500 and 503,000 barrels per day. These two refineries are 3.2% and 2.9% of total U.S. capacity. The top 62 with over 100,000 barrels per day capacity are 79.5% of U.S. capacity.

It is unfortunate that our refining capabilities are heavily concentrated in small areas. Because of close proximity, disruption of service would seriously impact the U.S. economy. Table VIa presents refining capacity by state. Texas has 26.9% of U.S. refining capacity and Louisiana 17% for a total of 43.9%. Most of this is on or near the Gulf Coast with major refining activity concentrated on the Houston Ship Channel. This area would be a major target for an enemy strike on the U.S. The area is also susceptible to hurricanes as evidenced by Katrina and Rita in recent years. The concentration of refineries on the Gulf Coast has come about because of production in the Southwest and Gulf of Mexico. Another factor has been proximity of supply to markets. Refineries in California, Illinois, Pennsylvania and New Jersey serve major population areas.

U.S. Refinery and Blender Net Production are presented in Table VIb. The distribution of products in this table is very revealing. Naphtha (ASTM No. 1), the feedstock for gasoline, makes up 46.5% of the output. Kerosene and Diesel fuels (ASTM No. 2) make up 31.5% for a total of 78% of the barrel of crude oil. The remaining portion of the barrel is divided into a variety of products ranging from low molecular weight gases (3.6%) to residual fuel oil (3.7%).

The No. 2 portion is divided into several different parts. The 15-ppm sulfur and under is for over-the-road trucks and the few Diesel automobiles in the U.S. The remainder of the Diesel is used in railroads, shipping, industrial and miscellaneous uses. Commercial aviation consumes 7.3% of the barrel of crude oil and military (mostly aviation) is 0.7% or about one-tenth of commercial aviation. In summary, transportation dominates the fuel usage from a barrel of crude oil.

Table VI
U.S. Refineries Operable Capacity
(Atmospheric Crude Oil Distillation Capacity as of January 1, 2007)

Rank	Company Name	Site	State	Barrels per day	Percent	Cumulative
1	ExxonMobil Refining & Supply	Baytown	TX	562,500	3.2%	3.2%
2	ExxonMobil Refining & Supply	Baton Rouge	LA	503,000	2.9%	6.1%
3	Citgo Petroleum Corp	Lake Charles	LA	429,500	2.5%	8.6%
4	BP Products North America Inc	Texas City	TX	417,000	2.4%	11.0%
5	BP Products North America Inc	Whiting	IN	410,000	2.4%	13.3%
6	ExxonMobil Refining & Supply	Beaumont	TX	348,500	2.0%	15.3%
7	Sunoco Inc (R&M)	Philadelphia	PA	335,000	1.9%	17.2%
8	Deer Park Refining Ltd	Deer Park	TX	333,700	1.9%	19.1%
9	Chevron USA Inc	Pascagoula	MS	330,000	1.9%	21.0%
10	WRB Refining LLC	Wood River	IL	306,000	1.8%	22.8%
11	Flint Hills Resources LP	Corpus Christi	TX	288,126	1.7%	24.4%
12	Motiva Enterprises LLC	Port Arthur	TX	285,000	1.6%	26.1%
13	Flint Hills Resources LP	Saint Paul	MN	279,300	1.6%	27.7%
14	Houston Refining LP	Houston	TX	270,200	1.5%	29.2%
15	BP West Coast Products LLC	Los Angeles	CA	265,000	1.5%	30.7%
16	Chevron USA Inc	El Segundo	CA	260,000	1.5%	32.2%
17	Premcor Refining Group Inc	Port Arthur	TX	260,000	1.5%	33.7%
18	Conocophillips Company	Belle Chasse	LA	247,000	1.4%	35.1%
19	Conocophillips Company	Sweeny	TX	247,000	1.4%	36.6%
20	Marathon Petroleum Co LLC	Garyville	LA	245,000	1.4%	38.0%
21	Chevron USA Inc	Richmond	CA	242,901	1.4%	39.4%
22	Motiva Enterprises LLC	Norco	LA	242,200	1.4%	40.7%
23	Conoco Phillips Company	Westlake	LA	239,400	1.4%	42.1%
24	ExxonMobil Refining & Supply	Joliet	IL	238,600	1.4%	43.5%
25	Conoco Phillips Company	Linden	NJ	238,000	1.4%	44.8%
26	Motiva Enterprises LLC	Convent	LA	235,000	1.3%	46.2%
27	Total Petrochemicals Inc	Port Arthur	TX	232,000	1.3%	47.5%
28	BP West Coast Products LLC	Ferndale	WA	225,000	1.3%	48.8%
29	Marathon Petroleum Co LLC	Catlettsburg	KY	222,000	1.3%	50.1%
30	Valero Refining Co	Texas City	TX	218,500	1.3%	51.3%
31	Flint Hills Resources	North Pole	AK	210,000	1.2%	52.5%
32	Conoco Phillips Company	Ponca City	OK	194,000	1.1%	53.7%
33	Chalmette Refining LLC	Chalmette	LA	192,760	1.1%	54.8%
34	Marathon Petroleum Co	Robinson	IL	192,000	1.1%	55.9%
35	Valero Refining Co	Norco	LA	185,003	1.1%	56.9%
36	Conoco Phillips Company	Trainer	PA	185,000	1.1%	58.0%
37	Premcor Refining Group Inc	Delaware City	DE	182,200	1.0%	59.0%
38	Premcor Refining Group Inc	Memphis	TN	180,000	1.0%	60.1%
39	Sunoco Inc	Marcus Hook	PA	178,000	1.0%	61.1%
40	Valero Energy Corporation	Sunray	TX	171,000	1.0%	62.1%
41	PDV Midwest Refining Llc	Lemont	IL	167,000	1.0%	63.0%
42	Tesoro Refining & Marketing Co	Martinez	CA	166,000	1.0%	64.0%
43	Sunoco Inc	Toledo	OH	160,000	0.9%	64.9%
44	Valero Refining Co	Paulsboro	NJ	160,000	0.9%	65.8%
45	Citgo Refining & Chemical Inc	Corpus Christi	TX	156,000	0.9%	66.7%
46	Shell Oil Products US	Martinez	CA	155,600	0.9%	67.6%
47	ExxonMobil Refining & Supply	Torrance	CA	149,500	0.9%	68.4%
48	Premcor Refining Group Inc	Lima	OH	146,120	0.8%	69.3%

Table VI (Continued)

Rank	Company Name	Site	State	Barrels per day	Percent	Cumulative
49	WRB Refining LLC	Borger	TX	146,000	0.8%	70.1%
50	Shell Oil Products US	Anacortes	WA	145,000	0.8%	71.0%
51	Sunoco Inc	Westville	NJ	145,000	0.8%	71.8%
52	Valero Refining Co	Benicia	CA	144,000	0.8%	72.6%
53	Valero Refining Co	Corpus Christi	TX	142,000	0.8%	73.4%
54	Conocophillips Company	Wilmington	CA	139,000	0.8%	74.2%
55	BP Products North America Inc	Toledo	OH	131,000	0.8%	75.0%
56	Western Refining Company LP	El Paso	TX	122,000	0.7%	75.7%
57	Murphy Oil Usa Inc	Meraux	LA	120,000	0.7%	76.4%
58	Tesoro West Coast	Anacortes	WA	120,000	0.7%	77.0%
59	Coffeyville Resources LLC	Coffeyville	KN	112,000	0.6%	77.7%
60	Frontier El Dorado Refining Co	El Dorado	KN	107,500	0.6%	78.3%
61	Marathon Petroleum Co LLC	Detroit	MI	100,000	0.6%	78.9%
62	Pasadena Refining Systems Inc	Pasadena	TX	100,000	0.6%	79.5%
63	Shell Oil Products US	Wilmington	CA	97,000	0.6%	80.0%
64	Conoco Phillips Company	Ferndale	WA	96,000	0.6%	80.6%
65	Tesoro Hawaii Corp	Kapolei	HI	93,500	0.5%	81.1%
66	Valero Energy Corporation	Three Rivers	TX	93,000	0.5%	81.6%
67	Valero Refining Co	Ardmore	OK	87,400	0.5%	82.1%
68	Sunoco Inc	Tulsa	OK	85,000	0.5%	82.6%
69	Navajo Refining Co	Artesia	NM	84,000	0.5%	83.1%
70	Valero Refining Co	Houston	TX	83,000	0.5%	83.6%
71	NCRA	McPherson	KN	81,200	0.5%	84.0%
72	Ultramar Inc	Wilmington	CA	80,887	0.5%	84.5%
73	Chevron USA Inc	Perth Amboy	NJ	80,000	0.5%	85.0%
74	Shell Chem LP	Saraland	AL	80,000	0.5%	85.4%
75	Valero Refining Co	Krotz Springs	LA	80,000	0.5%	85.9%
76	Calcasieu Refining Co	Lake Charles	LA	78,000	0.4%	86.3%
77	Conoco Phillips Company	Rodeo	CA	76,000	0.4%	86.8%
78	Marathon Petroleum Co LLC	Canton	OH	73,000	0.4%	87.2%
79	Marathon Petroleum Co LLC	Texas City	TX	72,000	0.4%	87.6%
80	Tesoro Alaska Petroleum Co	Kenai	AK	72,000	0.4%	88.0%
81	Sinclair Oil Corp	Tulsa	OK	70,300	0.4%	88.4%
82	Lion Oil Co	El Dorado	AR	70,000	0.4%	88.8%
83	Marathon Petroleum Co LLC	Saint Paul Park	MN	70,000	0.4%	89.2%
84	Alon USA Energy Inc	Big Spring	TX	67,000	0.4%	89.6%
85	Big West Of California	Bakersfield	CA	66,000	0.4%	90.0%
86	Sinclair Oil Corp	Sinclair	WY	66,000	0.4%	90.4%
87	United Refining Co	Warren	PA	65,000	0.4%	90.7%
88	Suncor Energy (USA) Inc	Commerce City	CO	62,000	0.4%	91.1%
89	ExxonMobil Refining & Supply	Billings	MT	60,000	0.3%	91.4%
90	Giant Yorktown Refining	Yorktown	VA	59,375	0.3%	91.8%
91	Conoco Phillips Company	Billings	MT	58,000	0.3%	92.1%
92	Delek Refining Ltd	Tyler	TX	58,000	0.3%	92.4%
93	Tesoro West Coast	Mandan	ND	58,000	0.3%	92.8%
94	Tesoro West Coast	Salt Lake City	UT	58,000	0.3%	93.1%
95	Placid Refining Co	Port Allen	LA	56,000	0.3%	93.4%
96	Cenex Harvest States Coop	Laurel	MT	55,000	0.3%	93.7%
97	Shell Chem LP	Saint Rose	LA	55,000	0.3%	94.0%

Table VI (Continued)

Rank	Company Name	Site	State	Barrels per day	Percent	Cumulative
98	Chevron USA Inc	Honolulu	HI	54,000	0.3%	94.4%
99	Wynnewood Refining Co	Wynnewood	OK	54,000	0.3%	94.7%
100	Paramount Petroleum	Paramount	CA	50,000	0.3%	95.0%
101	Petro Star Inc	Valdez	AK	48,000	0.3%	95.2%
102	Frontier Refining Inc	Cheyenne	WY	47,000	0.3%	95.5%
103	Chevron USA Inc	Salt Lake City	UT	45,000	0.3%	95.8%
104	Conoco Phillips Company	Arroyo Grande	CA	44,200	0.3%	96.0%
105	Calumet Shreveport LLC	Shreveport	LA	42,000	0.2%	96.2%
106	US Oil & Refining Co	Tacoma	WA	37,850	0.2%	96.5%
107	Hunt Refining Co	Tuscaloosa	AL	34,500	0.2%	96.7%
108	Murphy Oil USA Inc	Superior	WI	34,300	0.2%	96.9%
109	Edgington Oil Co Inc	Long Beach	CA	33,000	0.2%	97.0%
110	Citgo Asphalt Refining Co	Paulsboro	NJ	32,000	0.2%	97.2%
111	Suncor Energy (USA) Inc	Denver	CO	32,000	0.2%	97.4%
112	Big West Oil Co	North Salt Lake	UT	29,400	0.2%	97.6%
113	Citgo Asphalt Refining Co	Savannah	GA	28,000	0.2%	97.7%
114	Kern Oil & Refining Co	Bakersfield	CA	26,000	0.1%	97.9%
115	Holly Corp Refining	Woods Cross	UT	24,700	0.1%	98.0%
116	Little America Refining Co	Evansville	WY	24,500	0.1%	98.2%
117	Countrymark Cooperative Inc	Mount Vernon	IN	23,000	0.1%	98.3%
118	Ergon Refining Inc	Vicksburg	MS	23,000	0.1%	98.4%
119	Giant Refining Co	Gallup	NM	20,800	0.1%	98.6%
120	Ergon West Virginia Inc	Newell (Congo)	WV	20,000	0.1%	98.7%
121	Petro Star Inc	North Pole	AK	17,500	0.1%	98.8%
122	Giant Industries Inc	Bloomfield	NM	16,800	0.1%	98.9%
123	Gulf Atlantic Operations LLC	Mobile	AL	16,700	0.1%	99.0%
124	Conoco Phillips Alaska Inc	Kuparuk	AK	15,000	0.1%	99.1%
125	San Joaquin Refining Co Inc	Bakersfield	CA	15,000	0.1%	99.1%
126	Wyoming Refining Co	Newcastle	WY	14,000	0.1%	99.2%
127	Calumet Lubricants Co LP	Cotton Valley	LA	13,020	0.1%	99.3%
128	Age Refining Inc	San Antonio	TX	13,000	0.1%	99.4%
129	BP Exploration Alaska Inc	Prudhoe Bay	AK	12,500	0.1%	99.4%
130	Hunt Southland Refining Co	Sandersville	MS	11,000	0.1%	99.5%
131	Silver Eagle Refining	Woods Cross	UT	10,250	0.1%	99.6%
132	American Refining Group Inc	Bradford	PA	10,000	0.1%	99.6%
133	Greka Energy	Santa Maria	CA	9,500	0.1%	99.7%
134	Montana Refining Co	Great Falls	MT	9,500	0.1%	99.7%
135	Lunday Thagard Co	South Gate	CA	8,500	0.0%	99.8%
136	Calumet Lubricants Co LP	Princeton	LA	8,300	0.0%	99.8%
137	Cross Oil Refining & Marketing	Smackover	AR	7,200	0.0%	99.9%
138	Valero Refining Co	Wilmington	CA	6,300	0.0%	99.9%
139	Somerset Refinery Inc	Somerset	KY	5,500	0.0%	99.9%
140	Goodway Refining LLC	Atmore	AL	4,100	0.0%	100.0%
141	Silver Eagle Refining	Evanston	WY	3,000	0.0%	100.0%
142	Tenby Inc	Oxnard	CA	2,800	0.0%	100.0%
143	Foreland Refining Corp	Eagle Springs	NV	2,000	0.0%	100.0%
	U.S. Total			**17,443,492**		

U.S. Department of Energy, Energy Information Administration,
http://www.eia.doe.gov/neic/rankings/refineries.htm

Table VIa
U.S. Refining Capacity by State
(Atmospheric Crude Oil Distillation Capacity as of January 1, 2007)

Rank	State	Barrels per Day	Percent	Cumulative
1	Texas	4,685,526	26.9%	26.9%
2	Louisiana	2,971,183	17.0%	43.9%
3	California	2,037,188	11.7%	55.6%
4	Illinois	903,600	5.2%	60.8%
5	Pennsylvania	773,000	4.4%	65.2%
6	New Jersey	655,000	3.8%	68.9%
7	Washington	623,850	3.6%	72.5%
8	Ohio	510,120	2.9%	75.4%
9	Oklahoma	490,700	2.8%	78.3%
10	Indiana	433,000	2.5%	80.7%
11	Alaska	375,000	2.1%	82.9%
12	Mississippi	364,000	2.1%	85.0%
13	Minnesota	349,300	2.0%	87.0%
14	Kansas	300,700	1.7%	88.7%
15	Kentucky	227,500	1.3%	90.0%
16	Montana	182,500	1.0%	91.0%
17	Delaware	182,200	1.0%	92.1%
18	Tennessee	180,000	1.0%	93.1%
19	Utah	167,350	1.0%	94.1%
20	Wyoming	154,500	0.9%	95.0%
21	Hawaii	147,500	0.8%	95.8%
22	Alabama	135,300	0.8%	96.6%
23	New Mexico	121,600	0.7%	97.3%
24	Michigan	100,000	0.6%	97.9%
25	Colorado	94,000	0.5%	98.4%
26	Arkansas	77,200	0.4%	98.8%
27	Virginia	59,375	0.3%	99.2%
28	North Dakota	58,000	0.3%	99.5%
29	Wisconsin	34,300	0.2%	99.7%
30	Georgia	28,000	0.2%	99.9%
31	West Virginia	20,000	0.1%	100.0%
32	Nevada	2,000	0.0%	100.0%
	Total	**17,443,492**		

U.S. Department of Energy, Energy Information Administration,
http://www.eia.doe.gov/neic/rankings/refineries.htm

Table VIb
U.S. Refinery and Blender Net Production
Thousand Barrels per Day

	2002	2005	2007	
Total	17,273	17,800	17,963	
Liquefied Refinery Gases	671	573	647	3.6%
Ethane/Ethylene	25	20	20	0.1%
Ethane	19	13	14	0.1%
Ethylene	6	7	6	0.0%
Propane/Propylene	572	540	562	3.1%
Propane		311	330	1.8%
Propylene	225	229	232	1.3%
Normal Butane/Butylene	76	43	66	0.4%
Normal Butane	56	38	70	0.4%
Butylene	20	5	-4	0.0%
Isobutane/Isobutylene	-2	-30	-1	0.0%
Isobutane	-5	-31	-3	0.0%
Isobutylene	3	0	2	0.0%
Finished Motor Gasoline	8,183	8,318	8,344	46.5%
Reformulated	2,690	2,898	2,936	16.3%
Reformulated Blended w/ Ether		1,060	0	0.0%
Reformulated Blended w/ Alcohol		1,777	2,911	16.2%
Reformulated (Non-Oxygenated)		62	26	0.1%
Conventional	5,492	5,419	5,407	30.1%
Conventional Blended w/ Alcohol		961	1,237	6.9%
Conventional Other		4,458	4,171	23.2%
Finished Aviation Gasoline	17	17	16	0.1%
Kerosene-Type Jet Fuel	1,514	1,546	1,448	8.1%
Commercial	1,342	1,393	1,314	7.3%
Military	172	153	134	0.7%
Kerosene	57	66	35	0.2%
Distillate Fuel Oil	3,592	3,954	4,131	23.0%
15 ppm and under		23	2,842	15.8%
Greater than 15 ppm to 500 ppm	2,606	2,909	638	3.6%
Greater than 500 ppm	986	1,022	651	3.6%

Table VIb (Continued)

	2002	2005	2007	
Residual Fuel Oil	601	628	670	3.7%
Less Than 0.31 Percent Sulfur	72	76	81	0.5%
0.31 to 1.00 Percent Sulfer	143	142	136	0.8%
Greater Than 1.00 Percent Sulfur	386	410	453	2.5%
Petrochemical Feedstocks	392	389	399	2.2%
Naphtha For Petrochemical Feedstock	241	214	200	1.1%
Other Oils For Petrochemical Feedstock	150	174	198	1.1%
Special Naphthas	52	38	42	0.2%
Lubricants	174	168	178	1.0%
Naphthenic	34	27	28	0.2%
Paraffinic	140	141	150	0.8%
Waxes	17	16	12	0.1%
Petroleum Coke	781	835	824	4.6%
Marketable	543	596	584	3.3%
Catalyst	239	239	240	1.3%
Asphalt and Road Oil	492	512	455	2.5%
Still Gas	667	684	693	3.9%
Miscellaneous Products	62	59	69	0.4%
Fuel Use	7	0	2	0.0%
Nonfuel Use	56	58	67	0.4%
Processing Gain(-) or Loss(+)	-957	-989	-1,005	

U.S. Department of Energy, Energy Information Agency
http://tonto.eia.doe.gov/dnav/pet/pet_pnp_refp2_dc_nus_mbbl_m.htm

Appendix D

Fuel Use by Transportation Mode

In Appendix D, we will examine how much fuel is used in the various transportation modes and projected trends based on past usage.

Table VII presents transportation sector energy use from 2001 through 2008 in trillions of Btu's. It is more convenient to evaluate petroleum consumption in the more familiar units of million barrels per day. The two units are related by the following equation:

$$\text{Million barrels per day} \times 2{,}070 = \text{Trillion Btu's}$$

The last column gives the percent change between 2001 and forecast for 2008. These numbers are very revealing. Over this period, the statistics reveal a 19.7% total usage increase in automobiles and light trucks. Automobiles changed very little. However, light trucks increased by 47.4% tracking the increase of these vehicles on the road. Fuel usage by light commercial trucks increased by 12.8% and freight trucks by 13.1%.

During these years, fuel consumption by aviation is projected to increase by 6.9% with freight carriers making up most of the increase. Water transportation reduces by 2.0% and rail increases by 0.6%. The data show military use increasing by 23.1%. All of these predictions indicate enormous pressure on crude oil consumption and imports.

Table VIIa presents 2007 data in trillion Btu's and million barrels per day. Of 19.42 million barrels per day of oil consumed, 14.5 million barrels per day or 74.6% of the total oil was consumed in all forms of transportation including military. Highway use was 58% with automobiles and light trucks at 44.2% and commercial trucks and buses at 13.8%. Aviation was 7.7% and remaining non-highway use (including rail, water, pipelines and military) was 7.1%.

Overall, these data show an enormously disproportionate use in highway and aviation, 65.7%, compared with 7.1% for all other modes including water and rail. Let us now look at each of these transportation modes and consider their efficiencies.

LIGHT-DUTY VEHICLES

This category includes automobiles and trucks used in personal and business use. Table VIII gives the number of vehicles in this category compared with population and drivers from 1960 through 2003. There has been a tripling in the number of vehicles as the population has grown 61% from 180 to 291 million. The number of vehicles per person has almost doubled from 0.41 in 1960 to 0.79 in 2003. Based on fuel consumption in 2003, the average automobile consumed 584 gallons of fuel. Table VIIIa gives average vehicle mileage since 1960. Mileage improved from 13.3 mpg in 1980 to 16.4 mpg in 1990. There has been little improvement since. Based on average mileage in 2003, the average vehicle traveled about 10,000 miles per year.

COMMERCIAL TRUCKS

The number of trucks by weight on U.S. roads is given in Table VIIIb. This shows a 43.9% growth in the number of trucks from 1992 to 2002. It is logical to assume that this growth rate has been maintained through 2008. Trucks weighing less than 6,000 lbs. average between 15 and 20 mpg. Mileage decreases to about 5 mpg for 60 – 80,000 lb. vehicles. From 2001 to 2008, fuel consumption in commercial trucks has increased by about 15%.

In 2008, larger than 28,000 lb. trucks are expected to consume 1.9 million barrels per day of fuel. For an estimated 3,000,000 trucks in this category in 2008, this amounts to 27 gal. per day which seems a small number. At 6 mpg, this would be 162 miles per day on average. This number compares very well with the number of trucks used in less than 500 mile trips.

Table VIIIc gives the freight hauled by trucks, railroads, water and air. In 2000, trucks carried 78% of the tonnage and 60% of the ton-miles. Trucks carried 68% of the tonnage in less than 500 mile trips compared with 10% in over 500 mile trips. Ton-miles were 32% for over 500 mile trips and 28% for less than 500 mile trips. Trucks carried six times as many ton-miles in over 500 mile trips as railroads in competing intermodal service.

Railroads

Table VIIIc shows that railroads in 2000 carried 15% of the tonnage and 28% of the ton-miles of U.S. freight[1]. The dominant freight for railroads was coal (48%) in unit trains. The 2020 forecast is for 70% growth in total freight hauled compared to 2000 with about the same ratio between trucks and rail.

Table VIIId presents four railroad growth scenarios. If railroads spend $215 billion dollars in infrastructure investment by 2020, they will more than double intermodal freight. At the same time, the infrastructure investment for highways will be $1,900 billion.

Railroads can haul a ton of freight three times as far as a truck on the same amount of fuel. There are several reasons for this. More weight can be carried by a railroad freight car than an over-the-road truck. A railroad locomotive typically starts more slowly than a truck expending less energy to reach cruising speed. Railroads have very gentle grades compared with highways including freeways. Grades rarely exceed 2%. More importantly, highways have more frequent elevation changes than railroads. As a result, there is less energy expended to lift the weight of the train over mountainous terrain. Lastly, a train loses far less energy than a truck due to frequent accelerations and decelerations with braking.

Reciprocating Engines and Fuel Consumption

Spark-ignited (gasoline) and compression-ignited (Diesel) engines power most transportation modes with the exception of jet-powered aircraft. Reciprocating engines are inefficient devices that convert about 20% of the energy in the fuel into useable energy at the crankshaft. The basic reason for this is that the device is a large air compressor.

In four-stroke engines, air is compressed in the compression stroke. In two-stroke engines, air is compressed on each upward stroke. In either case, a large amount of power is consumed in this process. Many design changes have been made in engines to make them more efficient. Some examples are: overhead valves, increased valve size or increased number of valves, higher compression before ignition, fewer obstructions in the exhaust system, port and cylinder

---

[1] "Transportation: Invest in America, Freight-Rail Bottom Line Report," American Association of State Highway and Transportation Officials, Washington, DC, 2002.

fuel injection and turbochargers and superchargers to increase air mass in the cylinder. This leads to a fundamental conundrum; the larger the engine, the higher the fuel consumption. A 2.0 liter engine will always get lower fuel use than a 4.0 liter engine.

The next problem with American vehicles is weight. As with engines, many design changes have been made to improve efficiency such as air resistance. These changes are, at best, marginal. Unfortunately, physics controls fuel use. The larger the vehicle, the more energy is required to start it moving and accelerate. The equation is:

$$Energy = \tfrac{1}{2}\, mass \times velocity^2$$

The energy to reach a cruising speed increases by the square of the cruising speed.

Once a vehicle reaches cruising speed, air drag becomes a factor. The equation controlling this phenomenon is:

$$Energy = constant \times velocity^2$$

The energy to maintain 60 miles per hour is four times as great as the energy to maintain 30 miles per hour. The reason for the constant is the air drag coefficient which is a function of design.

Fuel consumption is reduced with lower speeds and less vehicle weight.

Table VII
Transportation Sector Energy Use by Mode and Type
Trillion Btu's

Energy Use by Mode	2001	2004	2007	2008	% Change 2001 - 2008
Highway					
Light-Duty Vehicles	15,161.1	16,472.8	17,761.0	18,145.3	19.7%
Automobiles	8,876.0	8,824.8	8,868.7	8,891.4	0.2%
Light Trucks	6,259.5	7,622.5	8,866.5	9,228.1	47.4%
Motorcycles	25.6	25.6	25.8	25.8	0.8%
Commercial Light Trucks	583.8	605.0	648.0	658.6	12.8%
Buses	251.1	242.3	248.7	250.7	-0.2%
Transit	98.9	95.5	98.0	98.8	-0.1%
Intercity	36.6	35.2	36.1	36.4	-0.5%
School	115.7	111.7	114.6	115.5	-0.2%
Freight Trucks	4,223.6	4,259.7	4,666.3	4,775.2	13.1%
Medium (1,000 - 26,000 lbs.)	692.1	697.6	740.1	750.4	8.4%
Large (> 26,000 lbs.)	3,531.5	3,562.1	3,926.2	4,024.8	14.0%
Non-Highway					
Air	2,966.8	2,786.3	3,076.0	3,171.1	6.9%
General Aviation	181.7	173.0	186.7	191.2	5.2%
Domestic Air Carriers	1,623.7	1,517.1	1,595.6	1,635.0	0.7%
International Air Carriers	564.6	518.9	576.9	593.8	5.2%
Freight Carriers	596.8	577.4	716.8	751.0	25.8%
Water	1,414.1	1,348.0	1,378.1	1,386.0	-2.0%
Freight	1,111.9	1,029.4	1,051.5	1,056.6	-5.0%
Domestic Shipping	338.4	317.5	335.5	339.4	0.3%
International Shipping	773.5	711.9	716.0	717.1	-7.3%
Recreational Boats	302.2	318.6	326.6	329.4	9.0%
Rail	616.2	588.4	616.6	620.1	0.6%
Freight	501.8	470.1	491.4	492.6	-1.8%
Passenger	114.3	118.3	125.2	127.5	11.5%
Intercity	26.3	26.9	28.5	29.0	10.3%
Transit	46.2	48.7	51.6	52.5	13.6%
Commuter	41.8	42.7	45.2	46.0	10.0%
Lubricants	194.0	200.4	205.5	208.2	7.3%
Pipeline Fuel Natural Gas	640.8	666.2	666.5	672.6	5.0%
Military Use	619.5	741.7	757.6	762.8	23.1%
Aviation	501.7	603.9	616.8	621.1	23.8%
Residual Fuel	18.3	21.9	22.4	22.5	23.0%
Distillate Fuel	99.5	115.9	118.4	119.2	19.8%
Total	26,671.0	27,910.8	30,024.3	30,650.6	14.9%

Department of Transportation, Energy Information Administration.
Table 2.1e Transportation Sector Energy Consumption, 1949-2006

Table VIIa
Transportation Sector Energy Use by Mode and Type

2007 Energy Use by Mode	Trillion Btu's	Million Barrels per day	Percent of Total Oil Consumed Primary Sectors	Breakdown Within Sectors	
Crude Oil and NG Liquids Consumed	40,190.0	19.415			
Highway	**23,324.0**	**11.268**	**58.0%**		
Light-Duty Vehicles	*17,761.0*	*8.580*		*44.2%*	
Automobiles	8,868.7	4.284		22.1%	
Light Trucks	8,866.5	4.283		22.1%	
Motorcycles	25.8	0.012		0.1%	
Commercial Light Trucks	*648.0*	*0.313*		*1.6%*	
Buses	*248.7*	*0.120*		*0.6%*	
Transit	98.0	0.047		0.2%	
Intercity	36.1	0.017		0.1%	
School	114.6	0.055		0.3%	
Freight Trucks	*4,666.3*	*2.254*		*11.6%*	
Medium (1,000 - 26,000 lbs.)	740.1	0.358		1.8%	
Large (> 26,000 lbs.)	3,926.2	1.897		9.8%	
Non-Highway	**5,942.9**	**2.871**	**14.8%**		
Air	*3,076.0*	*1.486*		*7.7%*	
General Aviation	186.7	0.090		0.5%	
Domestic Air Carriers	1,595.6	0.771		4.0%	
International Air Carriers	576.9	0.279		1.4%	
Freight Carriers	716.8	0.346		1.8%	
Water	*1,378.1*	*0.666*		*3.4%*	
Freight	1,051.5	0.508		2.6%	
Domestic Shipping	335.5	0.162			0.8%
International Shipping	716.0	0.346			1.8%
Recreational Boats	326.6	0.158		0.8%	
Rail	*616.8*	*0.298*		*1.53%*	
Freight	491.4	0.237		1.22%	
Passenger	125.2	0.060		0.31%	
Intercity	28.5	0.014			0.07%
Transit	51.6	0.025			0.13%
Commuter	45.2	0.022			0.11%
Lubricants	*205.5*	*0.099*		*0.5%*	
Pipeline Fuel Natural Gas	*666.5*	*0.322*		*1.7%*	
Military Use	**757.6**	**0.366**	**1.9%**		
Aviation	*616.8*	*0.298*		*1.5%*	
Residual Fuel	*22.4*	*0.011*		*0.1%*	
Distillate Fuel	*118.4*	*0.057*		*0.3%*	
Total	**30,024.5**	**14.505**			

Department of Transportation, Energy Information Administration.
Table 2.1e Transportation Sector Energy Consumption, 1949-2006

Table VIII
Vehicle and Population Ratios Since 1960

Year	Population	Drivers	Light-Duty Vehicles	% Growth	Vehicles per Person
1960	180	87	74		0.41
1965	194	99	90	4.65	0.46
1970	204	112	108	2.85	0.53
1975	215	130	133	2.31	0.62
1980	227	145	156	2.63	0.69
1985	239	157	172	3.61	0.72
1990	248	167	189	1.01	0.76
1995	263	177	202	2.02	0.77
2000	281	191	218	0.92	0.78
2001	281	191	226	3.66	0.80
2002	288	195	230	1.76	0.80
2003	291	196	231	0.43	0.79

All numbers in millions. Light duty vehicles include automobiles and light trucks.

U.S. Department of Transportation, Energy Information Administration.
http://www.bts.gov/publications/national_transportation_statistics/html/table_01_25.html

Table VIIIa

Average Vehicle Statistics

Year	MPG	Median Age, Years	
		Automobiles	Light Trucks
1960	12.4		
1965	12.5		
1970	12.0		
1975	12.2		
1980	13.3		
1985	14.6		
1990	16.4	6.5	
1995	16.8	7.7	7.4
2000	16.9	8.3	6.7
2004	17.1	9.0	6.6

U.S. Department of Transportation, Energy Information Administration.
http://www.bts.gov/publications/national_transportation_statistics/
html/table_01_25.html

Table VIIIb
Number of Trucks by Weight

	1992	1997	2002	Percent Change 1992-1997	Percent Change 1992-2002
All Trucks - Thousands	59,200.8	72,800.3	85,174.8	23.0%	43.9%
Light Trucks					
Less than 6,001 lb	50,545.7	62,798.4	62,617.3	24.2%	23.9%
6,001 to 10,000 lb	4,647.5	5,301.5	17,142.3	14.1%	268.8%
Medium Trucks					
10,001 to 14,000 lb	694.3	818.9	1,142.1	17.9%	64.5%
14,001 to 16,000 lb	282.4	315.9	395.9	11.9%	40.2%
16,001 to 19,500 lb	282.3	300.8	376.1	6.6%	33.2%
Light-Heavy Trucks					
19,501 to 26,000 lb	732.0	729.3	910.3	-0.4%	24.4%
Heavy Trucks					
26,001 to 33,000 lb	387.3	427.7	436.8	10.4%	12.8%
33,001 to 40,000 lb	232.6	256.7	228.8	10.4%	-1.6%
40,001 to 50,000 lb	338.6	399.9	318.4	18.1%	-6.0%
50,001 to 60,000 lb	226.7	311.4	326.6	37.4%	44.1%
60,001 to 80,000 lb	781.1	1,069.8	1,178.7	37.0%	50.9%
80,001 to 100,000 lb	33.3	46.3	68.9	39.0%	106.9%
100,001 to 130,000 lb	12.3	17.9	26.4	45.5%	114.6%
130,000 lb or more	4.6	5.9	6.3	28.3%	37.0%
Not reported	<50	<50	N	N	N

KEY: lb = pound; N = data do not exist.

NOTES
Average vehicle weight is the empty weight of the vehicle plus the average load of the vehicle. Excludes vehicles owned by federal, state, or local governments; ambulances; buses; motor homes; farm tractors; unpowered trailer units; and trucks reported to have been sold, junked, or wrecked prior to July 1 of the year preceding the 1992 and 1997 surveys and January 1, 2002 for the 2002 survey.

SOURCES
1992, 1997: U.S. Census Bureau, *1997 Economic Census: Vehicle Inventory and Use Survey: United States*, EC97TV-US (Washington, DC: 1999).
2002: U.S. Census Bureau, *2002 Economic Census: Vehicle Inventory and Use Survey: United States*, EC02TV-US (Washington, DC: 2004).

Table VIIIc
U.S. Domestic Freight

Year 2000	Tons Millions			Ton-Miles Billions			Miles per Ton
Truck Total	10,700		78%	2,639		60%	247
<500 Miles		9,339	68%		1,241	28%	133
>500 Miles		1,361	10%		1,398	32%	1,027
Rail	2,009		15%	1,239		28%	617
Bulk Commodities - Unit Trains		1,027	7%		582	13%	567
Industrial Commodies - Carloads		783	6%		421	10%	538
Containers - Intermodal Service		199	1%		236	5%	1,186
Water	1,054		8%	539		12%	511
Air	9		0.1%	9		0.2%	1,000
Total	13,772			4,426			321

Forecast Year 2020	Tons Millions			Ton-Miles Billions			Miles per Ton
Truck Total	17,296		80%	4,174		63%	241
<500 Miles		15,188	70%		2,046	31%	135
>500 Miles		2,108	10%		2,128	32%	1,009
Rail	2,891		13%	1,821		27%	630
Bulk Commodities - Unit Trains		1,294	6%		697	10%	539
Industrial Commodies - Carloads		1,268	6%		719	11%	567
Containers - Intermodal Service		329	2%		405	6%	1,231
Water	1,470		7%	617		9%	420
Air	25		0.1%	27		0.4%	1,080
Total	21,682			6,639			306

Transportation: Invest in America, Freight-Rail Bottom Line Report, John Horsley, Executive Director, American Association of State Highway and Transportation Officials, Washington, D.C., 2002.
http://www.freight.transportation.org/doc/FreightRailReport.pdf.

Table VIIId

Rail Growth Scenarios - 2020

Rail Infrastructure Investment	No Growth	Constrained	Base Case	Aggressive
		Ton Miles		
Rail				
Bulk Commodities - Unit Trains	582	697	697	697
Industrial Commodities - Carloads	421	463	719	965
Containers - Intermodal Service	236	371	405	603
Total Rail Freight	**1,239**	**1,531**	**1,821**	**2,265**
Truck				
<500 Miles	2,046	2,046	2,046	2,046
>500 Miles	2,128	1,993	1,959	1,761
Reduction by Intermodal Rail		6%	8%	17%
Total Truck Freight	**4,174**	**4,039**	**4,005**	**3,807**

	No Growth	Constrained	Base Case	Aggressive
		Billion $'s per Year		
Railroad Investment	115	155	185	215
Highway Investment	1,900	1,889	1,879	1,862
Shipper Costs	76.3	59.9	43.7	18.8

Transportation: Invest in America, Freight-Rail Bottom Line Report, John Horsley, Executive Director, American Association of State Highway and Transportation Officials, Washington, D.C., 2002.
http://www.freight.transportation.org/doc/FreightRailReport.pdf.

Appendix E

Reduction of Liquid Petroleum Fuel Consumption in Transportation

A large amount of data and information have been presented as background to understand sources of energy, our dependence on foreign energy and where it is used. In 2007, the U.S. used 101.4 quadrillion Btu's per year. We imported 29.4% of our total energy use: 25.6% as crude oil and 3.9% as natural gas. Natural gas is used to generate electricity and this will be addressed in Appendix F. The basic premise set forth has been to reduce fuel consumption by 20% and increase domestic oil production by 50% until alternative fuels can replace petroleum fuels. These are ambitious goals and may take years to achieve. An evaluation is given in this appendix of alternative fuels and other ways to reduce consumption of petroleum fuels.

The purpose of Table IX is to illustrate how the proposals presented in this book can bring down imports. The data begin with 2007 total domestic and imported oil consumed and its use in principle transportation areas. We consumed 19.42 million barrels per day and imported 12.97 million barrels per day. This does not count ethanol and Bio-Diesel as alternative fuels consumed.

In the second column, consumption in highway and air modes was reduced by 10%. Domestic production is increased to 10 million barrels per day and 1 million barrels per day of alternative fuels are added. The result is that imports decrease from 12.97 to 8.15 million barrels per day.

In the third column, consumption in highway and air modes was reduced by 20%. Domestic production is increased to our goal of 14 million barrels per day and 2 million barrels per day of alternative fuel are added. The result is that imports are reduced to 2.87 million barrels per day. Increasing alternative fuels to 4.87 million barrels per day would eliminate imports.

FEDERAL FUEL EFFICIENCY MANDATES

Development of more fuel efficient automobiles and trucks as mandated by federal law through 2020 will bring about sizeable savings. The current automobile and light-duty truck fleet averages about 17 mpg. Achieving 35 mpg in these vehicles would be equivalent to an overall 25% reduction in consumption reducing our dependence on foreign crude by 33%. This is based on the assumption that the population of vehicles in these categories does not increase and no alternative fuels are used.

ALTERNATIVE FUELS

There are a number of alternative fuel sources that are well known. Each has unique problems associated with it. The following is a review of these sources.

Liquid Fuels from Coal and Natural Gas

Conversion of coal into liquid fuels has been known since the beginning of the 20th century. The Fischer-Tropsch process was developed in the 1920's and used by Nazi Germany during World War II as a fuel source. The SASOL processes were developed and are now commercialized in South Africa. The last plant built in South Africa produces 150,000 barrels per day. There have been recent improvements on these processes in China. Liquid fuels can be made from natural gas in similar processes such as the Mobil Process.

Liquid fuels from coal and natural gas are compatible with the existing fuel infrastructure. These fuels are essentially refined products requiring no further refining capacity. New processes produce gas fuel from coal that can be used in electrical generation and hydrogen for use in specialized transportation applications. The cost to produce these fuels is in the $30-50 per barrel range.

Replacement of liquid fuel from petroleum with fuel from coal is a net zero offset of carbon dioxide. Liquid fuel from coal and natural gas is the most likely replacement for petroleum fuels.

Shale Oil

Shale oil is a fine-grained sedimentary rock containing kerogen, a solid mixture of organic compounds. There are large deposits around the world amounting to 2.8 to 3.3 trillion barrels of oil. The U.S. has 62% of these reserves.

Oil is recovered from shale by mining and then transported to an ex-situ location for processing. Kerogen is converted to crude oil through the process of pyrolysis, a process of heating to 450° C. (842° F.) in the absence of oxygen. This is obviously an energy intensive operation. The cost to extract oil from shale was $70 to $90 per barrel in 1970 dollars, about the current cost ($140 per barrel) of crude oil in 2008 dollars.

There are environmental considerations in the mining of shale oil and extracting the oil that are easily equal to the problems with tar sands. Shale oil has been described as the future source of crude oil, and that will always be in the future.

Tar Sands

Tar sands are a naturally occurring mixture of sand or clay, water and heavy crude oil. These sands occur throughout the world including the United States in limited amounts. The largest deposits are in Canada and Venezuela. Canada is the only country producing hydrocarbons from these sands on a commercial level.

Tar sands represent about two-thirds of all known hydrocarbon reserves; 3.6 trillion barrels in Canada and Venezuela alone compared with 1.75 trillion barrels of crude oil worldwide.

The problem with extracting the hydrocarbons is the environmental impact. The oil is extracted with in-situ methods such as cyclic steam stimulation and steam assisted gravity drainage. There is a large amount of byproduct in the form of clay, water and hydrocarbon that cannot be easily returned to the environment. Other methods include strip-mining and moving the product to an ex-situ location. A problem with this is transportation costs and energy consumption. The energy multiplier is currently 5 to 6 and expected to improve to 9:1 by 2015. The cost to produce a barrel of oil from tar sands is $40 - $50 in 2008 dollars.

In summary, the smaller deposits of tar sands in the U.S. do not lend this fuel to be a large scale replacement for foreign crude oil.

Bio-Diesel

Synthesis of fatty acid methyl esters (FAME) or Bio-Diesel is a small but active industry in the United States. There are two problems with Bio-Diesel. The first is obtaining a large scale source of raw materials. There are limited amounts of used motor oil, cooking fats and other waste products of this type. Virgin oil feedstock, rapeseed and soybean oil, are most commonly used; soybean oil alone accounts for about ninety percent of all fuel stocks in the U.S.

Bio-Diesel can also be obtained from field pennycress, jatropha and other crops such as mustard, flax, sunflower, palm oil, and hemp.[1]

The second problem is cost. Bio-Diesel has a tax abatement to offset the cost of about $3.25 per gallon to manufacture the product. Now that Diesel fuel prices are approaching $5.00 per gallon, it has become an economically viable fuel.

Ethanol

Although ethanol use has been mandated in gasoline in the U.S., it is a bad idea that cannot be sustained. Ethanol is produced from plants such as sugar cane and corn. Ethanol contains oxygen, reducing the heat content and fuel efficiency of vehicles. **The energy to produce ethanol is about equal to the energy it provides in fuel.** While it has been a boon to some farmers, use of ethanol has pushed up corn prices causing problems in poor countries for food costs. Ethanol is not a fuel that can be depended on in the future as a substitute for foreign crude oil.

It should be noted that substantial amounts of ethanol are consumed in Brazil where it is derived from cellulose sources. The U.S. has substantial tariffs on imported ethanol to encourage domestic production. While this might be a short-term solution to some fuel problems, it remains an imported fuel that we must avoid.

FUEL ADDITIVES

There are a number of fuel additives that have marginal to significant effects on fuel consumption. Fuel additives are not widely used for several reasons: engine manufacturers generally focus on engineering solutions versus fuel additives, the challenges associated with distribution and mixing with fuels, and boisterous claims that cannot be substantiated. Fuel additives that have been researched and properly formulated will improve fuel performance in the problem areas they are designed to address. With that thought in mind, we will look at different types of fuel additives, how they function and their effects on fuel consumption.

---

[1]http://en.wikipedia.org/wiki/Biodiesel

Metallic Combustion Catalysts

A number of metals have combustion catalyst characteristics. These include barium, calcium, iron, copper, manganese, cerium, platinum and palladium. Iron, cerium and platinum are available in commercial formulations. SFA International, Inc. discovered a synergistic effect between iron (Fe) and magnesium (Mg). The technology has been patented in thirty-three countries. This catalyst reduces fuel consumption between 6% for low emission Diesel (LED) fuel containing <15 ppm sulfur and 14% for 2% sulfur containing fuels. Several companies offer iron catalyst formulations. These products reduce fuel consumption by about 66% of SFA's Fe-Mg combination.[2]

Costs for these types of catalyst are usually no more than $0.05 to $0.06 per gallon. A 6% savings at $4.50 per gal. for Diesel fuel represents a **net** savings of $0.27 per gallon which is significant in today's markets.

It should be pointed out that to obtain EPA Registration for over-the-road use, extensive testing is required for metallic catalysts. This is to evaluate the metal oxides, where they reside following combustion, and their effect on engine wear and life. Off-road use (farm and construction equipment, railroads, tug boats, Diesel generator sets, etc.) does not require EPA testing.

Cetane Improvers

Cetane improvers reduce the flash point of Diesel fuel (or conversely, increase the vapor pressure) to improve combustion. These products yield a marginal mileage improvement and better cold starts.

Detergents

Oil companies generally add detergents to their high end gasoline products, i.e. premium fuel. The leader in this area is Chevron closely followed by Shell and Texaco. There is no doubt that these products clean the fuel system and injectors. As a result, fuel spray is even resulting in better burning. Vehicles that are built for low octane regular gasoline will benefit from an occasional tank of premium fuel to clean the fuel system.

---

[2] May, Walter R., "Hydrocarbon Fuel Combustion, Effect of Sulfur on Fuel Savings", American Chemical Society, Division of Fuels Chemistry, Philadelphia, PA, August 21, 2008.

Emulsifiers

An emulsifier is a chemical compound that causes two otherwise insoluble liquids to form a stable dispersion or emulsion. In fuel applications, emulsifiers are used to form stable suspensions of water in fuel oil.

One of the ways to reduce NOx in exhausts is to reduce combustion temperature. This can be done by introducing water into the fuel which cools the flame zone. Water is introduced to the fuel through emulsification.

The negative to introduction of water into fuel is heat loss required to vaporize water and convert it to superheated steam. This type of additive is generally used only in large boilers operating on residual oil or similar fuels.

Lubricity Agents

Federal and state regulations have pushed fuels toward much lower sulfur levels. Current regulations for on-road Diesel fuel are <15 ppm sulfur. To achieve this level, the fuel must go through a dehydrodesulfurization process in the refinery. The result is a breakdown of high molecular weight aromatic fuels that have a lubricating effect in the fuel. The result is a "dry" fuel that removes lubricating oils and can lead to galling or abrasion of metal parts such as fuel pumps, fuel injectors and valves in the fuel system. Lubricity agents are designed to replace some of this lubricating characteristic in the fuel. Lubricity agents burn well in the combustion process with minimal addition to smoke, soot and particulate matter in the exhaust.

Viscosity Modifiers

The viscosity of a fuel affects the spray pattern from injectors. This applies to port injection gasoline engines as well as cylinder injection Diesel engines. These products have more application in No. 2 grade fuels, i.e. Diesel, kerosene and jet fuels. Because of more efficient spray patterns, there are marginal improvements in fuel economy.

Octane Improvers

Fuels with higher vapor pressures tend to ignite from the heat of compression. In spark-ignited engines (gasoline) this is undesirable as ignition occurs before the piston reaches the peak of the stroke. This is called "knock" and can damage the engine. The problem can be solved in two ways: selection of lower vapor pressure hydrocarbons or use of an anti-knock agent. The 'knock' characteristic of a fuel led to devising the octane rating for gasoline. It is a simple comparison of engine operating characteristics between octane fuels, the eight carbon aliphatic hydrocarbon, C_8H_{18}, with other fuels.

About the time of World War II, the anti-knock characteristic of oil-soluble lead compounds was discovered. For the next 50 or so years, lead was used to control the octane number of gasoline. In the latter part of the 20th century, the poisonous characteristic of lead in exhaust gases was discovered. Lead use was immediately stopped. Since that time, octane has been controlled by blending of hydrocarbons in the refinery.

Following proscription of the use of lead in the U.S. and Canada, a product known as MMT or dicyclopentadienyl manganese (0) was used effectively in Canada to improve octane. That product has been phased out and is no longer used.

Table IX
Transportation Sector Fuel Use Reduction
Million Barrels per Day

Transportation Fuel Reduction	2007	10%	20%
Total Crude Oil and Fuel Consumed	19.42	18.15	16.87
U.S. Crude and NGL Production	6.45	10.00	14.00
Net Imports less Discrepancy	12.97	8.15	2.87
Alternative Fuels		1.00	2.00
2007 Energy Use by Transportation Mode			
Highway	11.27	*10.14*	*9.01*
Light-Duty Vehicles	8.58	*7.72*	*6.86*
Commercial Light Trucks	0.31	*0.28*	*0.25*
Buses	0.12	*0.11*	*0.10*
Freight Trucks	2.25	*2.03*	*1.80*
Non-Highway	**2.87**	***2.73***	***2.58***
Air	1.49	*1.34*	*1.19*
Water	0.67	0.67	0.67
Rail	0.30	0.30	0.30
Lubricants	0.10	0.10	0.10
Pipeline Fuel Natural Gas	0.32	0.32	0.32
Military Use	0.37	0.37	0.37
Total	14.50	13.24	11.96

Department of Transportation, Energy Information Administration.
Table 2.1e Transportation Sector Energy Consumption, 1949-2006

Table IXa

U.S. Energy Report

	Barrels per Day	$ per Year	Change Last Month	Last Year
Petroleum Consumption	19,420,000		0.5%	3.8%
Domestic Production	6,450,000		-1.5%	-8.5%
Foreign Imports	12,970,000	$662,767,000,000	1.85%	6.9%

Do your Part to Reduce Crude Oil Imports. Conserve Energy!

Stop the Flow of Money Out of Our Country

Appendix F

Electrical Power

Before we can formulate a long-term solution to transportation issues that will bring us to energy independence from foreign sources, we must look at electrical power that will play a significant part in that plan. Table X was discussed in Chapter 4 and provides insight into the cost of generating electricity by fuel and country.

Table Xa presents electrical power generation by fuel sources from 1993 through 2007. The percent numbers on the last row are for 2007. Almost one-half of our electrical power is generated with coal. Natural gas and nuclear power are about equal. Those three energy sources combined with hydroelectric make up about 95% of the energy used to generate electricity.

The U.S. electric power generation increased from 3,200 to 4,200 gigawatts in the period 1993 to 2007. While coal has grown by 25%, natural gas use has more than doubled and nuclear has grown by 33%. Hydroelectric has shrunk. This chapter discusses each of these energy sources.

COAL

The U.S. has the largest coal reserves of any country in the world: 246 billion tons of recoverable coal. This is equivalent to 1,088 billion barrels of oil compared to Saudi Arabia's 260 billion barrels of reserves. The entire world oil reserves are 1,317 billion barrels making U.S. coal reserves equal to 82.6% of the entire world's oil reserves in terms of energy. It is estimated that we have a 260-year supply of energy from coal at current use rates.[1]

The problem with coal is environmental pollution. While there will be more on this in Appendix G on hydrocarbon combustion chemistry, coal produces about 1.5 times as much carbon dioxide per Btu of power as does natural gas. While in this author's opinion the jury is still out on the influence of human beings on global climate change, we must be concerned about the rising carbon dioxide levels in the upper atmosphere. Carbon dioxide is necessary for plant life.

---

[1] Coal, http://en.wikipedia.org/wiki/Coal.

Unfortunately, forests are being cleared reducing consumption of carbon dioxide by plants. Absorption of carbon dioxide into ocean water will raise the pH of ocean water by altering the ratio of acid to salt in the natural carbonic acid – carbonate buffer. This buffer maintains a 7.6 to 7.8 pH in ocean water and cannot be disturbed without disastrous effects on ocean life.

There is technology to sequester carbon dioxide from coal-fired generating plants. This involves storing carbon dioxide underground or at extreme ocean depths where the pressure causes this gas to become liquid. Another problem with coal is that it contains some mercury, a highly poisonous heavy metal. The level of mercury in seawater and aquatic life from coal exhausts has raised issues about contaminating an important food source. It should also be pointed out that the exhausts from coal plants contain sufficient thorium to contaminant the surrounding area with more radioactive material than is found around nuclear power plants.

Because of these concerns, there is an increasing resistance to construction of new coal-fired electrical generating plants. This is not likely to abate in the near future. In addition, the value of coal as liquefied fuel may replace it as a low cost solid fuel for production of steam in an electrical power plant. The use of coal for electricity generation can be expected to decline in coming decades.

Natural Gas

Natural gas is a combination of methane, ethane, propane and butane, the four smallest molecules in the family of aliphatic hydrocarbons. It has a very high heat value because of the ratio of hydrogen to carbon in the molecule, CH_4, C_2H_6, C_3H_8 and C_4H_{10}. The heat value is about 22,000 Btu's per pound compared with 19,000 for Diesel fuel and 12-14,000 for coal.

Natural gas is generally found near oil fields. When it is initially produced, it contains some liquids that are higher molecular weight hydrocarbons and sulfur compounds. These byproducts are removed at processing plants. The result is a very clean fuel.

Natural gas is located all over the world. Table XI gives proven world reserves. Russia has the most reserves with the U.S. in fifth place. Thirty-nine countries have 98% of the reserves. Note that Canada is in 16th place with about one-fourth of the reserves of the U.S. We are currently importing from Canada about 16% of gas used in the U.S.

OPEC countries have about 51% of natural gas reserves, which is considerably less than the dominant position they have in petroleum reserves (Table XIa). This is mostly due to the enormous reserves in Russia.

Natural gas is located in 24 of the 50 states of the U.S. It is also located offshore and particularly in the Gulf of Mexico. Texas has 29% of U.S. reserves followed by Wyoming, New Mexico, Oklahoma, Colorado, Louisiana and Alaska. Those states with offshore reserves make up 82% of U.S. reserves.

Use of natural gas will increase for electricity generation. Coal plants will be slowly phased out. A revised transportation network will require a significant increase in electrical generation that replaces petroleum and other liquid fuels. It is expected that other energy sources will be needed in addition to natural gas to meet these future demands.

NUCLEAR POWER PLANTS

The purpose of this section is to discuss the availability of nuclear power and its potential as a future large source of electrical energy. More detailed discussion of nuclear power can be found in the article cited below.[2]

The development of energy from nuclear power plants began in the 1940's simultaneously with nuclear weapons development. The first nuclear power plants were constructed on pilot plant scales in the 1950's. The U.S. Navy developed nuclear power for submarines and aircraft carriers. Under the stringent demands of Rear Admiral Hyman Rickover, a stellar safety record has been achieved with no publicly known major incidents.

Nuclear power plants were constructed in the U.S. until about 1980. **The U.S. currently produces more nuclear power than any other country although France generates about 75% of its power with nuclear compared with 20% for the U.S.**

The Three Mile Island incident in 1979, which posed no risks to people, the movie "China Syndrome" and the Chernobyl disaster in 1986 led to irrational fears on the part of people and government. These two incidents effectively stopped nuclear power plant construction. Regardless of these two incidents, nuclear power remains one of the safest modes of power generation.

---

[2] Nuclear Power, Wikipedia, http://en.wikipedia.org/wiki/Nuclear_Power.

There are large quantities of uranium deposits all over the world and particularly in the U.S. Uranium is as common as tin and germanium and thirty-five times as common as silver. The U.S. had 'forward cost' reserves in 2003 at $50 per lb. of 424 tons.[3] It is estimated that these resources would last 80 years at current consumption rates. A doubling of this price would be expected to yield a ten-fold increase in reserves. The possibility of extracting uranium from less conventional sources such as granite and seawater becomes feasible at higher prices for uranium based fuel. In addition, fission reactions – combination of lighter elements into heavier elements - become viable leading to an unlimited supply of heavy water and deuterium from seawater.

The environmental aspects of nuclear power are both positive and negative. On the positive side, there are no carbon dioxide, particulate matter, carbon monoxide, nitrogen oxides or other emissions associated with combustion of hydrocarbons and coal. On the negative side, there is the problem of spent fuel. Untreated spent fuel contains nucleotides with half-lives up to 2,500 years. Further treatment will recover energy from these compounds and reduce half-lives so that the wastes are safe after 125 years. In both cases, there is a long-term problem with storage of nuclear wastes.

While there is much hysteria about radiation from nuclear power plants, in actual fact, the amount of radiation from a nuclear power plant is less than the radiation from the trace nucleotides in the exhausts of coal plants.

The ultimate nuclear energy source will be fusion power. This refers to fusing two light atoms to form a heavier nucleus and releasing energy in the process. Fuel – such as sea water – for this reaction is much more widely available than for fission reactions. This area of technology is not developed for practical use at this time. A lot of research and development will be needed to make this energy source commercially feasible.

In summary, the future of U.S. electrical power generation for at least the 21st century lies with nuclear power. Further research and development on problems such as extraction of uranium from minerals, safe operating environments and extraction of more energy from spent fuel are needed. The federal government must initiate new laws, regulations and economic stimulus plans to support construction of new and safe nuclear electrical power plants

---

[3] U.S. Uranium Reserves Estimates,
http://www.eia.doe.gov/cneaf/nuclear/page/reserves/ures.html.

to replace old coal plants and provide more energy for new modes of transportation.

HYDROELECTRIC AND PETROLEUM FUELS

Hydroelectric power sources have decreased from 280 to 248 gigawatts between 1993 and 2007. There is little prospect for much growth in this area as it has already been well developed.

Petroleum fuels have similar environmental problems as coal regarding release of carbon dioxide, particulate emissions and nitrogen oxides. Because of the cost of crude oil, they cannot compete with lower cost coal and natural gas. These energy sources will continue to reduce as a component in electrical power generation.

RENEWABLE SOURCES – WINDMILLS

There is currently a lot of interest in wind farms for generating electricity. There are many practical problems with this form of power generation. To begin, a windmill costs about $1,000,000 and produces one megawatt per hour. It has a sizeable footprint, about one acre. The result is a high initial investment. Newer design 2.5 megawatt windmills are 500 feet high and occupy 160 acres or one quarter of a square mile of land. The cost for these larger windmills is $2,500,000 without considering the land, installation or operation.

The next problem is the unreliability of power from these generators because of the vagaries of the weather. There are complaints from environmentalists concerning the effect on birds that fly into the blades. Lastly, there is the issue of the aesthetics of a wind farm. This author believes that wind farms for power generation will not be a large-scale solution to low cost, non-polluting renewable energy.

RENEWABLE SOURCES – SOLAR

Solar energy has the same undependable aspect of the weather as windmills. Solar panels need cloudless days with long periods of sunlight. No matter where one goes in the world, there are a maximum twelve hours of sunlight every day averaged over a year. Cloud cover reduces this further. Solar panels have possibilities for residential use, especially with development of better methods of storing energy.

One problem with solar panels is the amount of land required to collect the sunlight energy. This has been partially solved in Spain with mirrors arranged around towers. The heat is collected at the top of the tower and transported to boilers to generate steam to produce electricity via steam turbines.

Future power can come from solar power farms in space. Methodology will have to be developed to transport the power from space to earth.

Table X

Comparison of Electricity Generating Cost by Fuel and Country
U.S. Cents/kw-hr

	France 2003	UK 2004	Chicago, U.S. 2004	Canada 2004	Europe 2007
Nuclear	3.7	4.6	4.2 - 4.6	5	5.4 - 7.4
Coal		5.2	3.5 - 4.1	4.5	4.7 - 6.1
Gas	5.8, 10.1	5.9, 9.8	5.5 - 7.0	7.2	4.6 - 6.1
Wind Onshore		7.4			4.7 - 14.8
Wind Offshore		11			8.2 - 20.2

First 5 gas row figures corrected for Jan 2007 US gas prices of $6.5/GJ (second figure for France & UK columns is using EU price of $12.15/GJ).
Chicago nuclear figures corrected to $2000/kW capital cost. Canada nuclear shows figures for ACR, not Candu.
Currency conversion at June 2007.
http://www.world-nuclear.org/info/inf02.html

Table Xa
Net Electrical Generation by Principle Energy Source
(Thousand Megawatthours)

Period	Coal	Natural	Nuclear	Hydro Electric	Other Renewables	Petroleum Liquids	Petroleum Coke	Other	Other	Hydroelectric Pumped Storage	Total
1993	1,690,070	414,927	610,291	280,494	76,213	104,387	8,401	12,956	3,487	-4,036	3,197,191
1994	1,690,694	460,219	640,440	260,126	76,535	98,440	7,461	13,319	3,667	-3,378	3,247,522
1995	1,709,426	496,058	673,402	310,833	73,965	66,944	7,610	13,870	4,104	-2,725	3,353,487
1996	1,795,196	455,056	674,729	347,162	75,796	73,521	7,890	14,356	3,571	-3,088	3,444,188
1997	1,845,016	479,399	628,644	356,453	77,183	82,773	9,782	13,351	3,612	-4,040	3,492,172
1998	1,873,516	531,257	673,702	323,336	77,088	116,859	11,941	13,492	3,571	-4,467	3,520,295
1999	1,881,087	556,396	728,254	319,536	79,423	107,276	10,785	14,126	4,024	-6,097	3,694,810
2000	1,966,265	601,038	753,893	275,573	80,906	102,160	9,061	13,955	4,794	-5,539	3,802,105
2001	1,903,956	639,129	768,826	216,961	70,769	114,647	10,233	9,039	11,906	-8,823	3,736,644
2002	1,933,130	691,006	780,064	264,329	79,109	78,701	15,867	11,463	13,527	-8,743	3,858,452
2003	1,973,737	649,908	763,733	275,806	79,487	102,734	16,672	15,600	14,045	-8,535	3,883,185
2004	1,978,620	708,854	788,528	268,417	82,604	100,040	20,731	16,766	14,483	-8,488	3,970,555
2005	2,013,179	757,974	781,986	270,321	87,213	100,095	22,427	16,317	12,468	-6,558	4,055,423
2006	1,990,926	813,044	787,219	289,246	96,423	44,655	19,709	16,060	13,977	-6,558	4,064,702
2007	2,020,572	893,211	806,487	248,312	102,988	49,956	15,752	15,414	13,815	-6,994	4,159,514
	48.6%	21.5%	19.4%	6.0%	2.5%	1.2%	0.4%	0.4%	0.3%	0.2%	

Energy Information Administration, Form EIA-906, Form EIA-920, "Combined Heat and Power Plant Report."

Table XI
World Proved Reserves of Natural Gas, 2007

	Country	Trillion Cubic Feet	Percent	Cumulative
1	Russia	1,680.000	27.2%	27.2%
2	Iran	974.000	15.8%	42.9%
3	Qatar	910.500	14.7%	57.7%
4	Saudi Arabia	240.000	3.9%	61.5%
5	United Arab Emirates	214.400	3.5%	65.0%
6	United States	204.385	3.3%	68.3%
7	Nigeria	181.900	2.9%	71.3%
8	Algeria	161.740	2.6%	73.9%
9	Venezuela	152.380	2.5%	76.3%
10	Iraq	112.000	1.8%	78.1%
11	Kazakhstan	100.000	1.6%	79.8%
12	Turkmenistan	100.000	1.6%	81.4%
13	Indonesia	97.780	1.6%	83.0%
14	Norway	82.320	1.3%	84.3%
15	China	80.000	1.3%	85.6%
16	Malaysia	75.000	1.2%	86.8%
17	Uzbekistan	65.000	1.1%	87.8%
18	Egypt	58.500	0.9%	88.8%
19	Canada	57.946	0.9%	89.7%
20	Kuwait[6]	55.000	0.9%	90.6%
21	Libya	52.650	0.9%	91.5%
22	Netherlands	50.000	0.8%	92.3%
23	Ukraine	39.000	0.6%	92.9%
24	India	37.960	0.6%	93.5%
25	Australia	30.370	0.5%	94.0%
26	Azerbaijan	30.000	0.5%	94.5%
27	Oman	30.000	0.5%	95.0%
28	Pakistan	28.000	0.5%	95.4%
29	Bolivia	24.000	0.4%	95.8%
30	Trinidad and Tobago	18.770	0.3%	96.1%
31	United Kingdom	17.000	0.3%	96.4%
32	Yemen	16.900	0.3%	96.7%
33	Argentina	16.090	0.3%	96.9%
34	Thailand	14.750	0.2%	97.2%
35	Mexico	14.557	0.2%	97.4%
36	Brunei	13.800	0.2%	97.6%
37	Papua New Guinea	12.200	0.2%	97.8%
38	Brazil	10.820	0.2%	98.0%
39	Burma	10.000	0.2%	98.2%
	World Total	**6,182.692**		

Energy Information Administration, Dept. of Energy, U.S. Crude Oil, Natural Gas 2005 Annual Report, DOE/EIA-0216(2005) November 2006

Table XIa
World Proved Reserves of Natural Gas, 2007
OPEC vs. Non-OPEC

	Country	Trillion Cubic Feet	Percent	Cumulative
	OPEC Countries			
1	Iran	974.000	30.9%	30.9%
2	Qatar	910.500	28.9%	59.8%
3	Saudi Arabia	240.000	7.6%	67.4%
4	United Arab Emirates	214.400	6.8%	74.2%
5	Nigeria	181.900	5.8%	80.0%
6	Algeria	161.740	5.1%	85.1%
7	Venezuela	152.380	4.8%	89.9%
8	Iraq	112.000	3.6%	93.5%
9	Indonesia	97.780	3.1%	96.6%
10	Kuwait	55.000	1.7%	98.3%
11	Libya	52.650	1.7%	100.0%
	OPEC Countries Total	**3,152.350**	**51.0%**	
	Non-OPEC Countries			
1	Russia	1,680.000	55.4%	55.4%
2	United States	204.385	6.7%	62.2%
3	Kazakhstan	100.000	3.3%	65.5%
4	Turkmenistan	100.000	3.3%	68.8%
5	Norway	82.320	2.7%	71.5%
6	China	80.000	2.6%	74.1%
7	Malaysia	75.000	2.5%	76.6%
8	Uzbekistan	65.000	2.1%	78.8%
9	Egypt	58.500	1.9%	80.7%
10	Canada	57.946	1.9%	82.6%
11	Netherlands	50.000	1.6%	84.3%
12	Ukraine	39.000	1.3%	85.5%
13	India	37.960	1.3%	86.8%
14	Australia	30.370	1.0%	87.8%
15	Azerbaijan	30.000	1.0%	88.8%
16	Oman	30.000	1.0%	89.8%
17	Pakistan	28.000	0.9%	90.7%
	Non-OPEC Countries Total	**3,030.342**	**49.0%**	
	World Total	**6,182.692**		

Energy Information Administration, Office of Oil and Gas.

Table XIb
Natural Gas Reserves by U.S. State, 2006
Billion Cubic Feet

	State	Reserves	Percent	Cumulative
1	Texas	61,836	29.3%	29.3%
2	Wyoming	23,549	11.2%	40.5%
3	New Mexico	17,934	8.5%	48.9%
4	Oklahoma	17,464	8.3%	57.2%
5	Colorado	17,149	8.1%	65.3%
6	Federal Offshore	15,360	7.3%	72.6%
7	Louisiana	10,474	5.0%	77.6%
8	Alaska	10,245	4.9%	82.4%
9	Utah	5,146	2.4%	84.9%
10	West Virginia	4,509	2.1%	87.0%
11	Kansas	3,931	1.9%	88.9%
12	Alabama	3,911	1.9%	90.7%
13	Michigan	3,065	1.5%	92.2%
14	Pennsylvania	3,050	1.4%	93.6%
15	California	2,794	1.3%	94.9%
16	Virginia	2,302	1.1%	96.0%
17	Arkansas	2,269	1.1%	97.1%
18	Kentucky	2,227	1.1%	98.2%
19	Montana	1,057	0.5%	98.7%
20	Ohio	975	0.5%	99.1%
21	Mississippi	813	0.4%	99.5%
22	North Dakota	479	0.2%	99.7%
23	New York	363	0.2%	99.9%
24	Miscellaneous	138	0.1%	100.0%
25	Florida	45	0.0%	100.0%
	U.S. Total	211,085		

Energy Information Administration, Office of Oil and Gas.

Appendix G

Hydrocarbon Combustion Reaction Chemistry and Environmental Considerations

For the immediate decades ahead of us and possibly for the remainder of the 21st century, liquefied and gaseous carbon-containing fuels with high energy levels similar to petroleum fuels in use today will remain a prime source of energy for transportation. There are no alternatives on the horizon for these fuels in large trucks, aviation and water transportation. These fuels can originate from petroleum, coal, shale oil, tar sands or natural gas. The commonality among them is that they contain carbon and produce carbon dioxide and water as byproducts of combustion. The following will give the reader a better understanding of the chemistry of combustion.

HYDROCARBON COMBUSTION CHEMISTRY

Table XII presents the combustion chemistry for methane (natural gas), aliphatic hydrocarbon (low emission Diesel fuel or LED), aromatic hydrocarbon (kerosene and jet fuel) and carbon (coal). The reactions for each of these fuels with oxygen are presented as balanced equations with carbon dioxide and water as the products of reaction. In addition, air accompanying the oxygen and excess air are included to give total mass of exhaust. A variable for excess air has been included in the calculations.

Fuel Consumed

The quantity of fuel consumed is based on a steam generator. In the example in Table XII, a 500 MW (500,000 Kilowatt) boiler is used. Each of the fuels has two variables, Btu's per pound and percent reactant in the fuel. For this example, coal has about 75% carbon per unit weight and 15,500 Btu's per pound. Natural gas contains 93% methane with 22,000 Btu's per pound. From these values we can calculate the weight of fuel consumed per hour and carbon dioxide output.

A 500 MW boiler will consume 149,000 lbs. methane and produce 374,000 lbs. carbon dioxide. The same boiler will consume 211,500 lbs. coal and produce 581,000 lbs of carbon dioxide. Because of the lower cost of coal, the economics are in favor of coal. It is interesting to note that aromatic fuels consume 182,000 lbs. fuel and produce 612,000 lbs. carbon dioxide.

Table XIIa compares total liquid petroleum fuels, natural gas and coal from Table II. From Quadrillion Btu's per year of fuel consumed in the U.S. in 2007, fuel weight and carbon dioxide production were calculated using the formulas in Table XII. This shows that natural gas produces about two-thirds of the carbon dioxide produced by coal. Petroleum fuels produce more carbon dioxide than coal and natural gas together.

Similar calculations were made based on electrical generation in Table XIIa. In the generation of electricity, coal produces 3.5 times the amount of carbon dioxide as natural gas while producing 2.5 times the amount of electricity. Petroleum liquids and coke are minor portions of the fuel used and carbon dioxide produced.

Fuel Combustion Byproducts

Carbon Dioxide

The chemical equations and calculations in Table XII demonstrate that carbon dioxide will be produced in the combustion of any fuel containing carbon. The amount depends on the purity of the fuel and heat of reaction – Btu content on a weight basis. Fuels such as ethanol and Bio-Diesel also produce carbon dioxide. The presence of oxygen in the fuel molecule does not change the fact that carbon dioxide is always an end product of combustion of a fuel containing carbon.

The United States produced 60 trillion short tons of carbon dioxide from carbon energy sources in 2007. The only way to reduce carbon dioxide is to reduce the amount of carbon containing fuels used for energy. Reduction of hydrocarbon fuel use in mostly transportation applications by 3 million barrels per day will reduce carbon dioxide by 7 trillion tons of carbon dioxide per year or 12%. Replacement of nuclear energy in the generation of electricity will likewise reduce carbon dioxide generation. **If we double the current percentage of nuclear power plants and reduce coal by the same amount, this will reduce carbon dioxide from coal in electrical generation by 40% or 7 trillion tons. Those two actions total 14 trillion tons or one-fourth of our total carbon dioxide production.**

Green plants absorb carbon dioxide and require it for growth and sustenance. The action proposed would leave the U.S. a net exporter of oxygen and help to balance increased carbon dioxide production from India and China.

Nitrogen Oxides

Nitrogen oxides (NOx) are pollutants and contribute to ozone formation in the upper atmosphere. NOx is produced by reaction between atmospheric nitrogen and oxygen at high temperatures. Anything that lowers the temperature surrounding the combustion reaction or immediately following will reduce NOx formation. It is interesting to note that Bio-Diesel increases NOx formation because of high flame temperatures.

Some metallic combustion catalysts reduce NOx by as much as 10%. Much larger reductions are found by emulsifying water into fuel. The downside to this is loss of heat used in the vaporization of water and raising the temperature of the steam.

Particulate Matter

Particulate matter is soot or smoke in engine exhausts. This is unburned or partially burned fuel. It generally comes about through poor fuel to air ratios and engine maintenance issues. Soot particles are condensed aromatic hydrocarbons that are carcinogenic. Studies on rats on verges of interstate highways have shown a high incidence of lung carcinomas caused by Diesel exhausts.

Elimination of soot and smoke will improve fuel efficiency through more complete combustion. This can be done with better engine design and maintenance plus metallic combustion catalysts.

Unburned Hydrocarbons and Carbon Monoxide

Unburned hydrocarbons and carbon monoxide are the result of incomplete or less than complete combustion. These products indicate less fuel efficiency as less energy is extracted from the fuel. Unburned hydrocarbons are condensed, aromatic hydrocarbons similar to particulate matter with high carcinogenicity. Carbon monoxide is a poisonous gas.

More efficient combustion eliminates these byproducts. This can be achieved in boilers and process heaters by increasing excess air. However, excess air increases exhaust volume removing additional heat from the boiler reducing efficiency.

More complete combustion can be achieved with improved equipment design, maintenance and use of fuel additives.

Table XII
Steam Boiler and Process Heater Combustion Reactions

10% Excess Air

Methane

1	CH_4 +	2.0	O_2 +	7.47	Air +	0.95	Excess Air	→	1	CO_2 +	2	H_2O +	8.41	Air
	16.334		64.000		209.384		27.34			44.011		36.032		236.7

Aliphatic

1	CH_2 +	1.5	O_2 +	5.60	Air +	0.71	Excess Air	→	1	CO_2 +	1	H_2O +	6.31	Air
	14.173		48.000		157.038		20.50			44.011		18.016		177.5

Aromatic

1	CH +	1.25	O_2 +	4.67	Air +	0.59	Excess Air	→	1	CO_2 +	0.5	H_2O +	5.26	Air
	13.092		40.000		130.865		17.09			44.011		9.008		148.0

Carbon

1	C +	1.0	O_2 +	3.73	Air +	0.47	Excess Air	→	1	CO_2	0	H_2O +	4.21	Air
	12.011		32.000		104.692		13.67			44.011				118.4

Table XII (Continued)
Steam Boiler and Process Heater Combustion Reactions

Fuel Fuel Type				Natural Gas Methane	Diesel Fuel Aliphatic	Kerosene Aromatic	Coal Carbon
Boiler Horsepower =			670,511				
Boiler Kilowatts =			500,000				
BTU/Lb.				22,000	18,000	18,000	15,500
Boiler efficiency			52%				
BTU/Kw Hr.			6,558				
BTU/Hr.			3,278,846,154				
Fuel/Hr.	Lbs./Hr.			149,038	182,158	182,158	211,538
	Kg./Hr.			67,603	82,626	82,626	95,953
	Cu. Ft.			3,401,293			
Percent Compound				93%	100%	100%	75%
Gram Moles Fuel/Hr.				3,849,051	5,830,009	6,311,308	5,991,584
Exhaust	Lbs./Hr.			2,890,272	3,079,142	2,796,289	2,859,712
	Kg./Hr.			1,311,019	1,396,690	1,268,388	1,297,157
	BTU/Hr.			508,183,951	541,392,176	491,659,229	502,810,751
	Heat Loss			15%	17%	15%	15%
Exhaust	Volume/Hour						
		Liters/Hr.		1,532,282,018	1,115,652,653	907,337,971	699,023,288
		Cu. Meters/Hr.		1,532,282	1,115,653	907,338	699,023
Exhaust Temp.		°C.	250				
		°F.	482				
Exhaust Volume/Hr.		Cu. Meters		2,934,649	2,136,714	1,737,747	1,338,780
Lbs. CO_2 per Hour				373,461	565,666	612,365	581,343
Tons CO_2 per Hour				187	283	306	291
Increased ratio of carbon dioxide over Natural Gas					1.51	1.64	1.56

Elemental and molecular weights, element distribution in air: **Handbook of Chemistry and Physics**, 65th Edition, 1984, CRC Press, Inc., Boca Raton, FL.

Principles of reaction stochiometry: Sienko, Michell J. and Plane, Robert A., **Chemistry**, McGraw-Hill Book Company, Inc., New York, 1957.

Table XIIa

U.S. Fuel Use and Carbon Dioxide Production

2007 Energy Use	Btu's/Hr (Quadrillion)	Fuel Consumed (Weight, Billion Short Tons per Year)	Carbon Dioxide	
Total Energy				
Petroleum Fuels	40.19	9,708	30,148	51%
Coal	22.7	6,414	17,629	30%
Natural Gas	23.58	4,700	11,779	19%
Total			59,566	
Electric Power Generation				
Coal	13.25	3,744	10,290	76%
Natural Gas	5.85	1,166	2,922	22%
Petroleum Liquids	0.33	79.72	247.5	2%
Petroleum Coke	0.1	25.14	84.5	1%
Total			13,544	

Elemental and molecular weights, element distribution in air: **Handbook of Chemistry and Physics**, 65th Edition, 1984. CRC Press, Inc., Boca Raton, Florida

Principles of reaction stochiometry: Sienko, Michell J. and Plane, Robert A., **Chemistry**, McGraw-Hill Book Company, Inc., New York, 1957 and other college freshman chemistry texts.

Appendix H

Economic and Consumption Effects on Oil Prices

The recent increase in crude oil prices is troubling from several aspects. In this section, economic factors related to petroleum consumption will be examined to evaluate different factors affecting oil prices.

WORLD OIL CONSUMPTION

Consumption is increasing on a worldwide basis. Two countries with the largest populations, China and India, are adding automobiles and trucks at a rapid rate. These two countries have approximately 40% of the world's population. They have a fledging middle class that is growing rapidly. The result is that a relatively small growth in automobiles per person is a large increase in overall vehicle count and petroleum consumption.

WORLD OIL PRODUCTION

Production is currently at 85 million barrels per day. The Bush administration has tried valiantly to increase production in OPEC countries. While 60% of oil reserves are in OPEC countries, production is not well developed and these countries appear to be producing at their limits. There are projections that world oil production can increase to 120 million barrels per day. That will be difficult to achieve and require massive investment in infrastructure.

Growing consumption and limited production increases are a major factor in driving the increases in oil prices. Energy independence in the U.S. will take enormous pressure off demand – 14 million barrels per day.

DEVALUED U.S. DOLLAR

The U.S. balance of payments has been negative since 1970. Data presented in Table XIII show that the U.S. trade balance has had an accumulated $6.7 trillion dollars negative balance since 1960. While the 2007 U.S. gross domestic product was more than $14 trillion, the annual deficit of $6.7 trillion for 2007 is a significant portion of the GDP.

Table XIIIa presents domestic crude oil prices in nominal and inflation adjusted dollars and compares these with the value of the Euro and price of oil in Euros. The dollar has devalued about 15% against the Euro over the past year. The price of crude oil has doubled. While a devalued dollar is part of the increased price of oil, it does not account for the total increase.

The effect of oil imports on U.S. trade balance is presented in Table XIIIb. Actual data for 2002 through 2007 are compared with projections for 2008. The balance of payments has ranged between ($327) and ($466) billion not including oil. With oil, the balance of payments has been ($423) and ($759) billion. **With oil prices doubling, a balance of payments of ($1,013) billion is projected for 2008. This has to affect the U.S. dollar and further devalue it.**

This is a spiraling down problem. To maintain the U.S. economy and current crude oil requirements, increasing negative balances of payments will lead to an eventual collapse of the U.S. dollar and the economy. Oil prices of $200 per barrel and higher have been forecasted. That will lead to gasoline prices in the range of $6 – 8/gallon with similar costs for Diesel fuel. **This will have a major impact on the U.S. economy and could likely bring on a severe worldwide depression.**

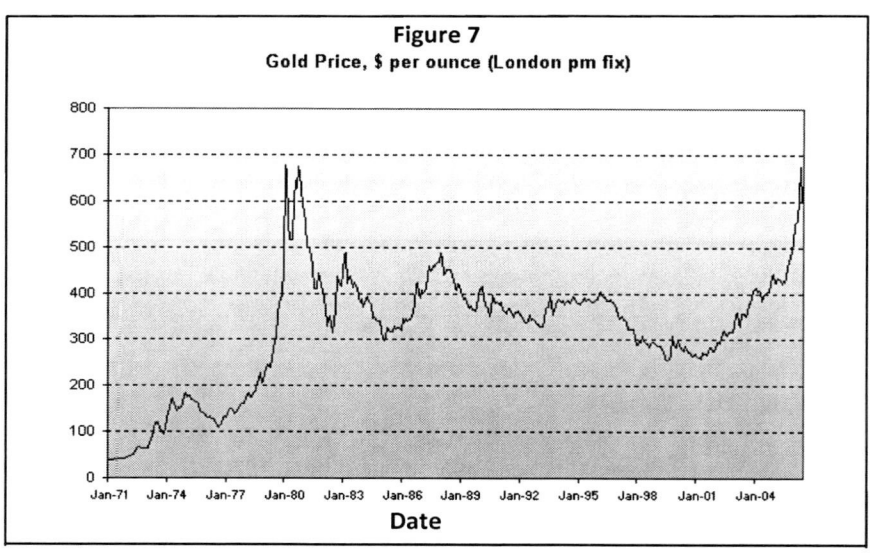

Figure 7
Gold Price, $ per ounce (London pm fix)

Gold

Figure 7 presents the price of gold in U.S. dollars since January 1971 when the U.S. dollar was removed from the gold standard. This chart is not inflation adjusted. In inflation-adjusted dollars, the dollar strengthened until 2001 and has devalued since that time.

Currencies

The conversion rate of Euros to U.S. dollars for the past ten years is presented in Figure 8. The dollar has devalued 36% against the Euro since 2001. The year 2001 was the turning point for dollars compared to both gold and the Euro. The U.S. negative balance of trade payments began to increase dramatically at the same time.

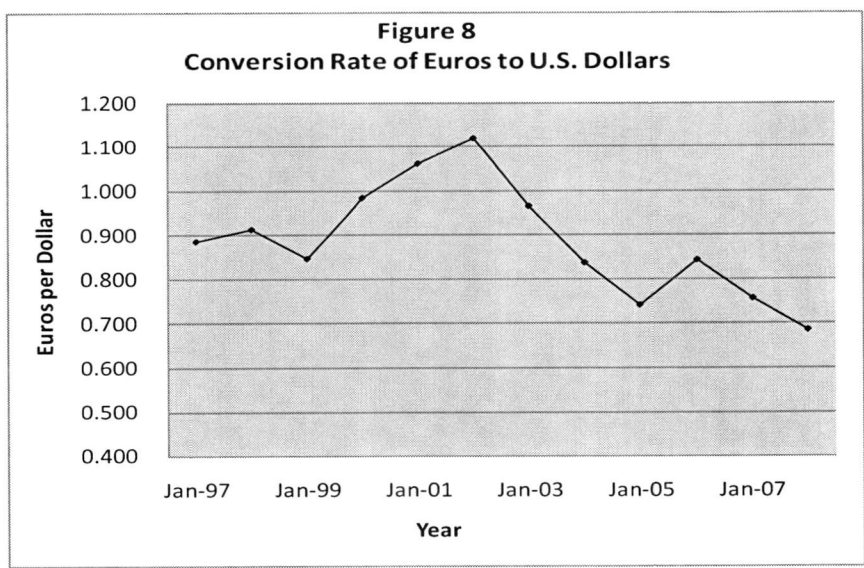

SPECULATORS

Speculation in the oil market has become headline news. The rise in crude oil prices in 2007 and 2008 has fueled rumor, fear and wild predictions. Faced with low interest rates and a declining stock market, large sums of money are being moved to markets with better opportunities for profit. Speculators are, in effect, hoarding through the futures commodity market and betting that the price of crude oil and petroleum products will continue to rise.

The way to reduce speculation is to establish a viable energy plan that will eliminate panic in the markets. Energy independence with all its economic benefits will promote price stability. The U.S. will regain control of the demand and supply of its energy.

Table XIII
United States Foreign Trade Balance
Millions of Dollars

Period	Balance of Payments			Exports			Imports
	Total	Goods	Services	Total	Goods	Services	Total
1960	3,508	4,892	(1,384)	25,940	19,650	6,290	22,432
1961	4,195	5,571	(1,376)	26,403	20,108	6,295	22,208
1962	3,370	4,521	(1,151)	27,722	20,781	6,941	24,352
1963	4,174	5,188	(1,014)	29,620	22,272	7,348	25,446
1964	6,022	6,801	(779)	33,341	25,501	7,840	27,319
1965	4,664	4,951	(287)	35,285	26,461	8,824	30,621
1966	2,939	3,817	(878)	38,926	29,310	9,616	35,987
1967	2,604	3,800	(1,196)	41,333	30,666	10,667	38,729
1968	250	635	(385)	45,543	33,626	11,917	45,293
1969	91	607	(516)	49,220	36,414	12,806	49,129
1970	2,254	2,603	(349)	56,640	42,469	14,171	54,386
1971	(1,302)	(2,260)	958	59,677	43,319	16,358	60,979
1972	(5,443)	(6,416)	973	67,222	49,381	17,841	72,665
1973	1,900	911	989	91,242	71,410	19,832	89,342
1974	(4,293)	(5,505)	1,212	120,897	98,306	22,591	125,190
1975	12,404	8,903	3,501	132,585	107,088	25,497	120,181
1976	(6,082)	(9,483)	3,401	142,716	114,745	27,971	148,798
1977	(27,246)	(31,091)	3,845	152,301	120,816	31,485	179,547
1978	(29,763)	(33,927)	4,164	178,428	142,075	36,353	208,191
1979	(24,565)	(27,568)	3,003	224,131	184,439	39,692	248,696
1980	(19,607)	(25,700)	6,093	271,634	224,050	47,584	291,241
1981	(16,172)	(28,023)	11,851	294,398	237,044	57,354	310,570
1982	(24,155)	(36,485)	12,330	275,236	211,157	64,079	299,391
1983	(57,768)	(67,102)	9,334	266,106	201,799	64,307	323,874
1984	(109,072)	(112,492)	3,420	291,094	219,926	71,168	400,166
1985	(121,880)	(122,173)	293	289,070	215,915	73,155	410,950
1986	(138,539)	(145,081)	6,542	310,033	223,344	86,689	448,572
1987	(151,683)	(159,557)	7,874	348,869	250,208	98,661	500,552
1988	(114,566)	(126,959)	12,393	431,149	320,230	110,919	545,715
1989	(93,141)	(117,749)	24,608	487,003	359,916	127,087	580,144
1990	(80,864)	(111,037)	30,173	535,233	387,401	147,832	616,097
1991	(31,135)	(76,937)	45,802	578,344	414,083	164,261	609,479
1992	(39,212)	(96,897)	57,685	616,882	439,631	177,251	656,094
1993	(70,311)	(132,451)	62,140	642,863	456,943	185,920	713,174
1994	(98,493)	(165,831)	67,338	703,254	502,859	200,395	801,747
1995	(96,384)	(174,170)	77,786	794,387	575,204	219,183	890,771
1996	(104,065)	(191,000)	86,935	851,602	612,113	239,489	955,667
1997	(108,273)	(198,428)	90,155	934,453	678,366	256,087	1,042,726
1998	(166,140)	(248,221)	82,081	933,174	670,416	262,758	1,099,314
1999	(265,090)	(347,819)	82,729	965,884	683,965	281,919	1,230,974
2000	(379,835)	(454,690)	74,855	1,070,597	771,994	298,603	1,450,432
2001	(365,126)	(429,519)	64,393	1,004,896	718,712	286,184	1,370,022
2002	(423,725)	(484,955)	61,230	974,721	682,422	292,299	1,398,446
2003	(496,915)	(550,892)	53,977	1,017,757	713,415	304,342	1,514,672
2004	(612,091)	(669,578)	57,487	1,157,250	807,516	349,734	1,769,341
2005	(714,371)	(787,149)	72,778	1,283,070	894,631	388,439	1,997,441
2006	(758,522)	(838,271)	79,749	1,445,703	1,023,109	422,594	2,204,225
2007	(708,515)	(815,369)	106,854	1,628,358	1,149,208	479,150	2,336,873
2008	(1,000,000)						
Totals	(7,415,969)	(7,777,585)	1,361,616	21,982,192	15,884,414	6,097,778	28,398,161

U.S. Census Bureau, Foreign Trade Division.
Data presented on a Balance of Payment (BOP) basis. Information on data sources and methodology are available at:
www.census.gov/foreign-trade/www/press.html.

Table XIIIa
Domestic Crude Oil Prices

Year	Dollars/Barrel Nominal	Inflation Adjusted	Euro/$	Euro/Bbl
1950	2.77	24.18		
1960	2.91	20.69		
1970	3.39	18.35		
1980	37.42	95.50		
1990	23.19	37.17		
1999	16.56	20.83	0.857	17.85
2000	27.39	33.39	0.993	33.16
2001	23.00	27.29	1.062	28.98
2002	22.81	26.61	1.122	29.86
2003	27.69	31.62	0.953	30.13
2004	37.66	41.84	0.795	33.26
2005	50.04	53.77	0.737	39.63
2006	58.30	60.73	0.845	51.32
2007	64.20	64.92	0.758	49.21
2008	125.00	125.00	0.680	85.00

U.S. Census Bureau, Foreign Trade Division.
www.census.gov/foreign-trade/www/press.html.

Table XIIIb
U.S. Oil Imports Cost

Year	2002	2003	2004	2005 Actual	2006	2007	2008 Projected
Million Bbls/Day	11.53	12.264	13.145	13.714	13.707	13.439	14
$/Bbl	22.81	27.69	37.66	50.04	58.3	64.2	120
Oil Imports, Million	$95,995	$123,950	$180,690	$250,481	$291,678	$314,916	$613,200
Balance of Payments	($423,725)	($496,915)	($612,091)	($714,371)	($758,522)	($708,515)	($1,013,200)
Net Imports less Oil	($327,730)	($372,965)	($431,401)	($463,890)	($466,844)	($393,599)	($400,000)

U.S. Census Bureau, Foreign Trade Division.
Data presented on a Balance of Payment (BOP) basis. Information on data sources and
methodology are available at www.census.gov/foreign-trade/www/press.html.

Glossary

Aliphatic	A class of organic compounds with the basic structure -CH_2- known as saturated compounds.
ANWR	Arctic National Wildlife Reserve
Aromatic	A class of organic compounds with the basic –CH- structure. The simplest example is benzene. Aromatic compounds are carcinogenic.
Asphaltenes	Condensed aromatic material occurring in petroleum products. They are aromatic in nature and generally contain sulfur.
API Gravity	An inverted density scale used by the U.S. petroleum industry. This scale can be related to density with the following equation:

$$\text{Density (gms/cu. cm.)} = 141.5 / (131.5 + API)$$

An API gravity of 10 is a density of 1. (Water free of air has a density of 1.000 gm/cc at 3.98° C.) Higher API gravities are lower density. An API gravity of 40 is 0.825 gm/cc.

ASTM	American Society of Testing and Materials. This organization sets procedures and standards for testing products across a wide range of industries.
Barrel	A unit of measurement for petroleum fluids. It is equal to 42 U.S. gallons.
Bio-Diesel	Fuel produced from fats and naturally occurring oil. The fuel is a fatty acid methyl ester (FAME). This fuel can be used in Diesel engines replacing ASTM No. 2 fuel or distillates. Because the raw materials used to manufacture the fuel are

	biogenic, it is known as Bio-Diesel, sometimes spelled biodiesel.
Biogenic	Products produced by life processes. Ethanol made from corn is a biogenic product.
Blender Net Production	The amount of product produced by a refinery that is available for consumer use.
Btu	British Thermal Unit. A Btu is the energy required to heat one pound of water one degree Fahrenheit.
Cafe Standards	Corporate Average Fuel Economy (CAFE) is the sales weighted average fuel economy, expressed in miles per gallon (mpg), of a manufacturer's fleet of passenger cars or light trucks with a gross vehicle weight rating (GVWR) of 8,500 lbs. or less, manufactured for sale in the United States, for any given model year. Fuel economy is defined as the average mileage traveled by an automobile per gallon of gasoline (or equivalent amount of other fuel) consumed as measured in accordance with the testing and evaluation protocol set forth by the Environmental Protection Agency (EPA).
Carbon Dioxide	The product of complete reaction in the combustion process of combining carbon with oxygen. The molecule, CO_2, contains one atom of carbon and two atoms of oxygen.
Carbon Monoxide	A product of incomplete reaction in the combustion process of combining carbon with oxygen. The molecule, CO, contains one atom of carbon and one atom of oxygen. It emulates the oxygen molecule, O_2, replacing it in tissue and causes death from oxygen starvation.
Catalyst	A compound that changes the rate of a chemical reaction. A catalyst can increase or decrease the rate of a reaction.

Centigrade	A temperature scale used with the metric system. In this scale, water melts at 0° and boils at 100°. The scale was devised by Anders Celsius in the early 18th century and is sometimes referred to as the Celsius temperature scale.
Cetane Improver	An additive that raises the vapor pressure of Diesel fuel making it easier to burn.
Coal	A carbon-containing solid fossil fuel. The U.S. has the largest coal deposits in the world. Coal can be used to manufacture liquid hydrocarbon fuels.
Combustion Catalyst	An additive containing oil-soluble metals that improves combustion. These products increase the rate of the combustion reaction resulting in more complete combustion and improved fuel efficiency. Some additives can also reduce particulate matter (smoke) and NOx.
Crude Oil	Petroleum fluid as it comes from the ground. Crude oil is the product of decomposition of organic matter from plants and animals.
Deuterium	Hydrogen has a molecular weight of 1.008. One neutron has a weight of 1.000. The reason for this difference is the presence of a very small amount of an isotope of hydrogen containing one proton and one neutron in the nucleus with an atomic weight of two. Because of the unusual properties of hydrogen with an atomic weight of two, the isotope has been given the name deuterium.
Diesel	Refers to Rudolph Diesel, 19th century inventor of the compression-ignited reciprocating engine. These types of engines are referred to as Diesel engines. The word Diesel should be capitalized as it refers to a proper name.
Diesel Fuel	A fuel within the ASTM No. 2 classification. This fuel has a lower vapor pressure and higher

Distillate	boiling range than No. 1 fuel and is used in Diesel engines.

Product that evaporates with heat and (sometimes) vacuum to form higher vapor pressure, low density products. In the petroleum industry, this refers to all products removed from crude oil by distillation. |
| Emulsifiers | An emulsifier is a chemical compound that causes two otherwise insoluble liquids to form a stable dispersion or emulsion. In fuel applications, emulsifiers are used to form stable suspensions of water in fuel oil.

Soaps and detergents are examples of emulsifiers. |
Engine Knock	Premature fuel ignition in the engine cylinder before the piston reaches the apogee and spark ignition is initiated. This can cause loss of power and fuel efficiency as well as engine damage.
Ethanol	An alcohol with the formula CH_3CH_2OH. This is the alcohol present in alcoholic beverages.
Ex-Situ	*Latin,* Out of its original place.
Export FAS	Refers to Free Alongside Ship – Product price includes shipment from the manufacturing plant to the dock ready for loading on a ship.
Fahrenheit	A temperature scale devised by Gabriel Daniel Fahrenheit, a German physicist. In this scale, water melts at $32°$ and boils at $212°$. It was thought at the time the scale was invented that $0°$ and $100°$ were the extreme temperatures that could be found in nature.
Fischer-Tropsch	A catalyzed chemical reaction in which synthesis gas, a mixture of carbon monoxide and hydrogen, is converted into liquid hydrocarbons of various

	forms. The most common catalysts are based on iron and cobalt, although nickel and ruthenium have also been used. The principal purpose of this process is to produce a synthetic petroleum substitute, typically from coal, natural gas or biomass, for use as synthetic lubrication oil or as synthetic fuel. This synthetic fuel is used in trucks, cars, and some aircraft engines.
Fission	The splitting of heavy elements into lighter elements with the release of energy following Einstein's law of energy, $E = MC^2$.
Flash Point	A test to measure the temperature a liquid ignites from a flame. The most common test is known as "closed cup". The liquid is in a cup with a gas flame over the liquid. The liquid is heated until it ignites. That temperature is the flash point. Liquids that ignite under 62° C. or 140° F. are rated hazardous for shipping purposes.
Fusion	The combining of lighter elements into heavier elements to form an unstable isotope and release of energy.
Gasoline	A high vapor pressure fuel with a low ignition temperature used in spark-ignited engines. It is formulated from naphtha or ASTM No. 1 feed stock.
Heavy Water	Water normally contains two atoms of hydrogen (containing one proton and one electron) and one atom of oxygen with a molecular weight of 18. Heavy water consists of oxygen with two atoms of deuterium and a molecular weight of 20,
Henry Hub	A standard for pricing natural gas. It is the price of natural gas in Erath, LA. This is similar to prices for Diesel fuel and gasoline at the New York Harbor.

High Speed Rail	Passenger trains that are powered with electricity and generally operate at speeds in excess of 150 mph.
Hybrid Vehicle	A vehicle with an electric drive. The electricity is supplied by a reciprocating engine powering a generator and batteries for electricity storage.
Hydrocarbon	A class of organic compounds containing hydrogen and carbon.
Hydrogen	The smallest atom containing one electron and one neutron. The molecular weight is 1.008. Hydrogen occurs in nature as the dimer, H_2.
In Situ	*Latin*, In its original place.
Intermodal	Combining modes of transportation. The term generally refers to trains carrying 20 foot and 40 foot ocean going containers on flat cars (COFC) and/or trailers (normally pulled by truck tractors) on flat cars (TOFC).
Kerogen	The organic material in shale oil. This material is broken down by pyrolysis or heating to recover the hydrocarbon product.
LED	Low Emission Diesel, a term referring to recently regulated fuels with ultra low levels of sulfur in the United States. Typical fuel for over-the-road vehicles contains less than 15 ppm sulfur.
Light Rail	A train with composite construction lighter than the typical passenger train. Designed for transport in populated areas and powered by electricity. The term *light rail* is preferred over *tram* when there is significant off-street travel. LRVs typically run along exclusive or semi exclusive rights-of-way. For efficiency, some LRVs preempt traffic signals.

LNG	Liquefied Natural Gas or natural gas in the liquid state. It is liquefied by reducing temperature and/or increasing pressure.
Lubricity	A characteristic of fuel referring to its ability to lubricate metal parts. Aliphatic fuels such as gasoline (naphtha) and LED fuels generally have low lubricity causing galling (abrasion) of moving metal parts in the fuel system.
Mag-Lev Trains	Magnetic Levitation trains that are elevated above the rail bed by a magnetic field. These trains travel up to 300 mph.
Methane	The most simple of alcohols. The formula is CH_3OH. Methanol is highly poisonous if consumed although it is widely used as an antiseptic.
Minemouth	Refers to coal prices at the entrance to the mine. These prices do not include any transportation costs.
Molecular Weight	The sum of the weights of the atoms in a molecule.
Naphtha	ASTM No. 1 grade fuel. This has the lowest boiling point range and highest vapor pressure of petroleum fuels. It is the feedstock used in manufacturing gasoline for spark-ignited engines.
Natural Gas	Low molecular weight aliphatic hydrocarbons ranging from methane to butane. Natural gas occurs in conjunction with crude oil.
NIMBY	Not In My Back Yard
Nitrogen Oxides (NOx)	Mixtures of compounds containing nitrogen and oxygen. These gasses contribute to air pollution.
No. 2 Fuel	Refers to ASTM classification of fuels. This group includes Diesel fuel, jet fuels and kerosene. No. 2

	fuel contains the higher boiling fractions from atmospheric distillation.
Non-OPEC	Countries that do not belong to the Organization of Oil Exporting Countries.
Nuclear Energy	Refers to energy coming from the fusion or fission of atomic nuclei.
Octane Number	A measure of the rate at which hydrocarbon fuels burn. Some hydrocarbons burn faster causing pre-ignition or 'knocking' in spark-ignited engines. Octane number of a fuel is a comparison to pure normal-octane as 100.
Off-Road Diesel	ASTM No. 2 fuel used in Diesel engines for non-highway purposes. In the U.S. today with LED regulations, it is generally the same as On-Road LED fuel. It is not taxed as are transportation fuels. It contains a dye, generally red, to identify it as untaxed fuel.
OPEC	The Organization of Oil Producing Countries. They are Algeria, Angola, Ecuador, Indonesia, Iran, Iraq, Kuwait, Libya, Nigeria, Qatar, Saudi Arabia, United Arab Emirates and Venezuela.
Particulate Matter	A product of incomplete reaction in the combustion process. It is synonymous with soot or smoke. It is generally measured as milligrams per cubic meter of exhaust. It is carcinogenic and results in lung carcinomas in laboratory rats on verges of highways. Combined with sulfuric acid from sulfur in the fuel, it prevents cloud formation.
Pyrolysis	A chemical reaction occurring at very high temperatures, generally in excess of $500°$ F or $260°$ C.

Refined Petroleum	Petroleum products that have passed through the refining process and separated into various boiling point fractions.
Residual Oil	ASTM No. 6 fuel. This is the residuum remaining after vacuum distillation.
SASOL	A South African company involved in mining, energy, chemicals and synthetic fuels. In particular, they produce petrol and Diesel fuel profitably from coal and natural gas using the Fischer-Tropsch synthesis. SASOL is an acronym in Afrikaans for *Suid-Afrikaanse Steenkool en Olie* - South African Coal and Oil.
Shale Oil	Oil from shale, a geological formation found in the western U.S. It is rock containing kerogen, an oil-containing structure.
Specific Gravity	The ratio of the mass of a volume of material to the mass of the same volume of water at 3.98° C. Specific gravity has no units.
Spent Fuel	Waste fuel from nuclear reactors. This fuel, without further treatment, contains radio nucleotides with high energy and long half-lives. Untreated fuel can be dangerous to life for up to 2,500 years. Spent fuel can be further processed recovering energy and reducing the time for safe return to the environment to 125 years.
Streetcar	A rail-born vehicle of lighter weight and construction than a train. It is powered by electricity and designed for the transport of passengers in close proximity. The tracks primarily run on streets. The Modern Streetcar is a fixed guide way electric rail system that operates at street level in mixed traffic. Name often interchanged with Tram and Trolley.
Sulfur	A chemical element present in petroleum fuels that combines with oxygen in the combustion

	process to form sulfur oxides. SO_3 combines with water to form H_2SO_4 or sulfuric acid, also known as acid rain.
Tar Sands	Petroleum deposits containing a high level of sand. There are large deposits in Canada and Venezuela and smaller deposits in the U.S.
Ton	A short ton is 2,000 pounds, a unit used in the United States. A long ton is 2,200 pounds, a unit used in Great Britain. A metric ton is 1,000 kilograms or 2,204.6 pounds, a unit used in countries on the metric system.
Tons Hauled	For commercial trucks, tons hauled refers to the gross number of tons hauled by trucks, regardless of distance.
Ton-Miles	For commercial trucks and railroads, ton-miles refer to tons times miles hauled.
Trailer	A large commercial truck rig consists of a tractor and trailer. A trailer is generally 40' in length, hauls a net weight of 40,000 lbs. and has an empty weight of 10,000 lbs or more.
Trans-Texas Corridor	A 4,000 miles system incorporating toll and non-toll highways; freight, high-speed passenger, regional passenger and commuter rail lines; water, oil and gas pipelines; electric transmission lines; and broadband and other telecommunication infrastructures.
Viscosity	A measure of the ability to pour or the thickness of a liquid. Viscosity is measured with the energy to stir the material or time to pour through a standard opening.

Bibliography

Articles and other sources are referenced in footnotes throughout the text and tables. The following resources provided the author with the comprehensive information presented in this book.

Chapter 2

The Wall Street Journal. Source of daily prices for petroleum products, natural gas, precious metals and currencies, international reports and energy information.

Chapter 3

American Association of Railroads, www.aar.org.

American Trucking Association, www.truckline.com.

Transportation: Invest in America, Freight-Rail Bottom Line Report, John Horsley, Executive Director, American Association of State Highway and Transportation Officials, Washington, D.C., 2002. http://freight.transportation.org/doc/FreightRailReport.pdf.

Wikipedia Encyclopedia. Source of general information on a variety of subjects.

Chapter 4

The Economics of Nuclear Power, www.world-nuclear.org/info/inf02.html

Appendices A through F

U.S. Department of Energy, Energy Information Agency: url http://eia.doe.gov.

Appendix G

Constants, atomic and molecular weights:

CRC Handbook of Chemistry and Physics, Ed. By R. C. Weast, CRC Press, Inc., Boca Raton, FL, 1985.

Physical Chemistry:

Moelwyn-Hughes, E. A., Physical Chemistry, Pergamon Press, London, 1957.

Dykstra, C. A., Physical Chemistry - A Modern Introduction, Prentice Hall, Upper Saddle River, NJ, 1997.

Physics:

Giancoli, D. C., Physics - Principles with Applications, Prentice Hall, Upper Saddle River, NJ, 1998.

Stochiometry:

Hutchinson, Eric, Chemistry. The Elements and Their Reactions, W. B. Saunders Company, Philadelphia, PA, 1959.

Sienko, M. J., Plane, R. A., Chemistry, McGraw-Hill Book Company, Inc., New York, 1957.

Combustion Catalysis and Treatment of Ash-Bearing Fuels:

SFA International, Inc., www.SFAInternational.com, 'Library' page.

Appendix H

U. S. Census Bureau, www.census.gov.

The Author

Walter May received a B.S. degree from Memphis State University in chemistry and mathematics and a Ph.D. degree from Vanderbilt University in chemistry and physics. He has published thirty technical papers, listed as inventor on twenty-three patents and contributed chapters for reference books. He was combustion turbine fuels editor for ***TurboMachinery International*** magazine from 1987 to 1992.

The author has worked in the petroleum industry since 1966. He has made major contributions to the technology of using unrefined crude oil and other ash-bearing fuels in combustion turbines, boilers and process heaters, and Diesel engines. This technology is widely used in oil-producing countries with minimal refining capacity to fuel combustion turbines with unrefined crude oil for the generation of electricity.

In his research, the author discovered a synergistic combination of iron and magnesium with unusual combustion catalyst properties. This catalyst reduces fuel consumption in Diesel engines by as much as 14% in high sulfur-containing fuels. Particulate matter is reduced in combustion turbine and process heater exhausts by 90% compared with 50% reported in the literature. The catalyst reduces NOx in engine exhausts.

In 1980, Walter was co-founder of SFA International, a manufacturer of oil-soluble metal compounds used in the formulation of liquid petroleum fuel additives. Currently, he serves as president of SFA International, Inc., Houston, Texas.

Walter May also serves as president of Walter May & Associates, a consulting firm knowledgeable in many aspects of petroleum fuel combustion processes. This company also provides expert witness testimonials in legal matters. Dr. May is available for lectures and speaking engagements. He has been invited to share his knowledge at seminars throughout the world.

Walter and his wife, Cheryl, reside in Houston, TX where they take great joy in spoiling grandchildren. He is a member of the American Chemical Society, Sigma Xi Research Fraternity, American Society of Mechanical Engineers, National Oil-Equipment Manufacturers and Delegates Society (NOMADS) and Houston Grampian Association – a petroleum focused sister city organization with Aberdeen, Scotland. Walter is active in Grace Presbyterian Church, a member of the Speakers Committee of the Houston Livestock Show and Rodeo™ and Past Chieftain and Treasurer of the Heather and Thistle Society. Walter's passion is music. He is a classically trained concert pianist and Rachmaninoff's concertos are his favorites. Walter enjoys giving benefit performances for charity and church organizations.

The author may be contacted at WMay@SFAInternational.com.

LaVergne, TN USA
15 October 2010
200963LV00001B/1/P